THE
COLLEGE GRACES
OF
OXFORD
AND
CAMBRIDGE

THE
COLLEGE GRACES
OF
OXFORD
AND
CAMBRIDGE

COMPILED BY

REGINALD H. ADAMS

Bodleian Library
UNIVERSITY OF OXFORD

This edition first published in 2013 by
the Bodleian Library
Broad Street

Oxford OX1 3BG

www.bodleianbookshop.co.uk

ISBN 978 1 85124 083 8

Text © Bodleian Library, University of Oxford, 2013
First published in 1992 by The Perpetua Press, Oxford,
as *The College Graces of Oxford and Cambridge*, by Reginald H. Adams
Cover image © Mei Chan

Cover design by Dot Little
Designed and typeset in 11 on 13 point Bembo Book
by illuminati, Grosmont
Printed and bound by Page Bros Ltd, Norwich, on 80gsm Munken Print Cream

British Library Catalogue in Publishing Data
A CIP record of this publication is available from the British Library

CONTENTS

HOC MUNUSCULUM
MARGARETAE
CONJUGI AMABILISSIMAE
PER QUINQUAGINTA ET QUINQUE
ANNOS BEATOS
GRATO ANIMO DONAT COLLATOR

✦

FOREWORD
TO THE FIRST EDITION

In 1989 S.J. Mitchell, Fellow Commoner of Christ's, made a collection of the college graces of Cambridge, and a similar study began in Oxford. The interest which this work aroused seemed to make desirable joint publication of the Latin texts with English translations. Sadly John Mitchell died a year later, but as his Oxford partner I was encouraged to pursue the idea with the great advantage of the careful preparatory work he had done in Cambridge. To this his wife and his friend and colleague at Christ's, Henry Button, both readily agreed. At that stage Hugo Brunner and Vivian Ridler of the Perpetua Press helpfully came forward to make publication possible, with the subsequent editorial aid of Neil Scott and the useful advice of Robin Birch and Julian Dare.

This book is concerned only with the Latin graces to be heard in the colleges of the two oldest universities in England, but they are of course found in other places of education and learning and in some religious societies and civic guilds. Praise be to God that so much has survived in such variety. In an age when the language, spoken or written, is under threat the continuation of ancient usage lends support to the study of Latin and the belief in its cultural importance. There are happily now indications of the desire to retain those ceremonies which our predecessors thought proper and which have been for so long part of the corporate life of a college.

Thanks are due to many in both universities who have supported with friendly encouragement and the supply of texts and information.

R.H.A.

DEO GRATIAS AGAMUS

THE GIVING OF THANKS at mealtimes has been a tradition in the universities since the foundation of the earliest colleges. The first reference to grace in any of their statutes is found among those which the Scottish princess Dervorguilla, as its co-founder, composed for Balliol in 1282,[1] ordaining 'that our scholars shall commonly speak Latin'. There was a clear provision that *singulis etiam diebus, tam in prandio quam in coena, dicant benedictionem antequam comedant, et post refectionem gratias agant* – 'every day both at dinner and supper they shall say a benediction before they eat, and after the meal they shall give thanks'. Such thanksgiving would have been customary in the Augustinian hospital of St John, from which the first college to be founded in Cambridge originated about the same time, Peterhouse. Some three and a half centuries later in the interest of reinforcement of discipline a reminder was included in the statutes of Pembroke College, Oxford,[2] founded in 1624, that no one would be allowed to begin eating before the first grace was said or to leave the hall until the concluding grace was pronounced on penalty of a fine. After seven hundred years it is still a treasured custom for each college to have a grace in the ancient tongue, used either *ante cibum* or *post cibum*.

Thanksgiving 'before meat' is of ancient origin. There are several references to the custom in classical literature and pious pagans offered libations to the deities. The Greeks provided a word for thanksgiving – 'Eucharist' and from the Latin tongue is derived 'gratitude'. *Gratiae* in the plural has become 'grace' in its singular form. Acknowledgement of divine bounty is more directly the inheritance of Jewish monotheism and feasts in the Old Testament are preceded by the blessing of a sacrifice. It was to be expected that the practice should be followed in Christ's ministry. Jesus blessed the bread and the fishes before the feeding of the multitude. St Paul, who had already written of thanksgiving as the sanctification of a meal, urged the brethren at Corinth when eating or drinking to do it to the glory of God.[3]

The wording of graces reflects the subsequent development of Christian worship. The basis of them all is the sacerdotal language of monastic prayer which survived the Reformation with its beauty enhanced in the Renaissance. It is possible to see a transition from brief benediction through lengthy thanksgiving returning in this age to graces which are not so long as to be tedious, yet traditional and telling. They are thus still to be heard as a suitable expression of the gratitude of academic communities in halls where their historical beauty and significance are appropriate.

The surviving corpus of Latin graces includes those said before and after meals. Those for use at the main meal of the day were entitled *ante prandium* and *post prandium*. Some colleges had other formulae known as *ante coenam* and *post coenam* for the supper meal. In such a way four graces could be acquired, and from the evidence at Christ's of a broadsheet,[4] which refers in the prayers to King Charles I, this seems not to have been unusual in the middle of the seventeenth century. Another change emerged with special graces before the beginning and at the end of feasts. A different set of four graces could thus be acquired, two of them ferial for everyday use and two festal.

The tradition of wearing gowns at dinner has also been preserved, the alumni of some Cambridge colleges having their own distinctive pattern.

Gratiarum actio

The summons to dinner at New College was until about 1830 made by two choristers who, starting from the gateway, proclaimed in unison, so prolonging the syllables that they lasted until reaching the hall – *Tem–pus vo–can–di à man–ger O seign–eurs* (Time to call you to dine my masters).[5] A chorister continues to play a part at Magdalen by intoning at feasts as *aularius* the announcement of 'Grace' with the words *Gratiarum Actio*. At The Queen's the summons is still by the sound of the trumpet, but apart from these Oxford oddities the tolling of the chapel bell is the normal signal for the start of dinner in hall.

'Hall', which once referred to the large chamber for meals with adjacent buttery, or sometimes was the name of the whole foundation, as at Trinity Hall and St Edmund Hall, has come to be used for attendance at dinner. A 'formal hall', which was threatened by the introduction of self-service meals, has survived as an essential part of community life, although an alternative meal without the formalities of dining and the wearing of gowns is usually provided.

Silence is obtained with the sounding of a gong or use of the gavel at High Table, in the past by the striking together of two wooden trenchers, and all stand. Though the head of the house or a presiding fellow sometimes pronounces it, the daily grace is often the responsibility of a scholar, and in one college at least it is included among the duties of a Bible clerk. In some a scholar is appointed to serve for the week as *lector hebdomadarius*.

There are now fewer undergraduates with any knowledge of Latin but fortunately it is still possible to find those willing and able to declaim grace with effect, either by reading from a text, which in some colleges is affixed to a board with a projecting handle, or *memoriter*. Appropriate dress and posture add to the dignity of the occasion. Pronunciation is in the style of reformed classical Latin, and efforts to break the record for rapid reading are nowadays less frequent. On the other hand, more careful preparation is evident, and the printing of the texts with a few vowel quantities marked where there might be reason for doubt, and with words spaced in lines of irregular length to suggest punctuation, is helpful. The Dean or the Chaplain is often the source of welcome support, and the regular grace is sometimes included in the termly chapel card for those who like to have the original and its translation at hand.

One of the features of monastic worship is the antiphonal voicing of versicles and responses such as is practised in the separation of cathedral choirs into *Decani* (the Dean's side) and *Cantoris* (that of the Precentor). As will appear, an antiphonal pattern in the saying or singing of grace is happily still to be found in one college in Oxford, University, and one in Cambridge, Trinity.

The *lector* used to remain for the after-dinner grace which is said at High Table. Soon after Benjamin Jowett became Master of Balliol in 1870, at a time of reform in the universities, he decided that this was no longer necessary at his college.[6] The 'Reminiscences' of a contemporary scholar at Trinity describe the resentment felt about this duty in Cambridge since it involved waiting in a draughty passage until the dons had finished their dinner.[7] But there is a reminder each night of past ceremonial in that college in the continuation of the custom of a rose-water bowl and ewer being presented by the butler at High Table as a signal of readiness for grace. Further reference to such customs will be found in an appendix of additional but not unrelated material.

Gratiae ante cibum

Those said before food, which have come to be known as 'college graces' and are the most frequently heard, can be roughly divided, as in the collection which follows, into one group which has its origin in the liturgy of the Church, and another of graces of more distinctive style which were composed mostly after the Reformation.

The earliest known form of grace is found in an eighth-century manuscript of the Gelasian Sacramentary.[8] It may have been composed well before its inclusion in this liturgical manual for the purpose it has since served as a collect at table. Though there are minor variations in wording, it has long been used as part of the grace at several colleges in Oxford and at a majority of the historic colleges in Cambridge, where a second petition was added at a later date. This ancient benediction is recognisable by its opening words – *Benedic Domine dona tua*.

The next most commonly found type of grace is an inheritance from mediaeval monasteries. Thence was derived the *Benedictio*

Mensae, which is still included in the Roman Catholic Breviary.[9] Henry Bradshaw, the eminent ecclesiastical historian and the university librarian at Cambridge until his death in 1886, made the point that all the college graces seemed 'to contain traces of the old groundwork... a psalm and a lesson or *capitulum* (brief extracts from the Bible) with the invocation of the *Kyrie*, the Lord's Prayer and the collect for the blessing' of the table.[10] The *capitulum* includes appropriate verses from the Psalms or sentences from the New Testament, and these contribute the second source of wording for grace. The chief components of the shortened graces which were adopted or adapted *in usum discipulorum* were a combination of the *capitulum* and the benediction collect.

The third kind of standard grace has an antiphonal pattern, each of the six lines being taken from a different Psalm, starting with *Benedictus sit Deus in donis suis.*

Some graces from these three sources are included in a section of graces found in the Consuetudinary for Salisbury Cathedral in the thirteenth century – the 'Use of Sarum'.[11] It was upon these statutes and customs that the first English Prayer Book was based, and thus a close link was established in liturgy and language between Roman and Anglican worship.

Graces as such did not officially find a place in the new Book of Common Prayer, but they were subsequently included in an edition for use in Christ Church, which is both cathedral and college.[12] An anthology of those in contemporary existence is found among a book of *Preces privatae* (*benedictiones mensae*) *in studiosorum gratiam collectae.*[13] From this it is clear which graces could have been in use at the time of the Elizabethan settlement. Apart from such a dividing line it remains almost impossible to assign any date to the first use of a specific text in any college. It cannot be assumed that any grace goes back as far as the time of foundation and it is known that changes have taken place. There is hardly any documentary evidence in college archives upon a subject about which it may have been assumed that there was little to be discussed.

The considerable similarity between the older graces could not easily have been avoided in wording hallowed by sacred origin and worship. This is especially true among some twenty of the oldest colleges, which were founded primarily for the education of the clergy. The graces in collect form of some sixteenth-century foundations, however, display a fresh theological approach, in particular with reference to the word of God as heavenly food and spiritual strengthening. Nourishment of mind as well as body is emphasised, and piety and learning are regarded as the most important part of our inheritance.

Similarity in another sense is apparent, because the words of Latin graces seem strangely familiar. 'For what we are about to receive' – 'For these and all His mercies may God's holy name be praised'. What are memories for many of the days of their youth are recognisable as translations of the earlier texts, and this speaks of the continuity of the faith.

It is perhaps remarkable that with the foundation of new colleges new compositions should be appearing in Latin. These are of especial interest, combining as they do the beauty of the ancient language with petitions appropriate for the present age. Their arrival is significant at a period which has seen a challenge to formality and a decline in the continuing use and teaching of Latin. The even greater threat, however, that of dissatisfaction with the principle of saying grace and with its Christian expression, may now perhaps have receded. It is certainly less vocal and it has been shown in one college in each university that conscientious objection can be satisfied with neat solutions. Modern compositions not only reflect the ancient wording but consider what is appropriate for all those who wish to acknowledge indebtedness.

A two-word blessing appeared, or reappeared, in the middle of the nineteenth century – *Benedictus benedicat* – 'May the Blessed One give a blessing'. The words in themselves may be regarded certainly as undenominational and possibly without commitment to religious belief. It is clear that their introduction created a turning point in tradition. They were also welcomed as an alternative to long preambles at meals, the length of which, it was argued, not only lessened appreciation of their literary quality but had a deterrent effect upon attention. More to the point the dinner might be getting cold. For these reasons this short formula became very popular, particularly in Oxford. Its brevity may perhaps give an impression of perfunctory ritual, though the two words are sometimes followed by the ascription *per Jesum Christum Dominum nostrum*. Despite expectations no liturgical precedents have been found for this euphonious grace. The origin of this way of consecrating a meal will be further discussed below.

Gratiae post cibum et festales

There remain to be considered the historic graces after meat and some specially composed for festal occasions. For the most part the latter are post-Elizabethan, though they reflect the traditional features of thanksgiving and rogation which characterise all earlier examples.

These elaborate and sometimes lengthy graces after meat, which were designed for daily use, almost without exception praise the Founder of the college concerned and usually its benefactors. A pattern was set in the original statutes for Balliol which coupled with the provision for grace a requirement for prayers 'for the souls of all our predecessors', already customary as the liturgical commemoration of the faithful departed. A toast is sometimes included in the ceremonial of a dinner 'to their pious memory'. There is close correspondence also with the special prayers, sometimes spoken in Latin, in Chapel at Evensong, especially at gaudies (*gaudeamus* – 'let us rejoice'), which echo the words of the graces in praise of founders and in some cases numerous benefactors.

The other feature in common in postprandial graces is that they generally consist of two supplications, the first for the Church and the sovereign in that order, a prayer which is the source of the SCR toast of 'Church and Queen'. There is frequent inclusion of the royal family, who at Trinity in Cambridge are listed in order of precedence, and once of parliament, at

Jesus there. The second supplication is for peace and unity in the Church and kingdom, sometimes widened to include peace for all Christian people. At St Catharine's, Cambridge a petition for truth is added to that for international peace, indicating contemporary concern about relations with foreign powers.

Sadly these examples of elegant and periodic Latin have rarely been heard in many colleges since their daily recital began to lapse a century ago when there ceased to be any formal conclusion to the evening meal. But in each university are to be found examples of the continuing use of the ancient postprandial grace. It is said each night after dinner in St John's in Cambridge, and during vacations in the Senior Combination Room. At Oxford Jesus has found the opportunity for its rhythmical *post cibum precatio* to be said at two or three special dinners each term for its graduate members. When those at High Table are ready to withdraw to the Senior Common Room it is the appropriate moment for the grace, which includes a versicle and response in which both reader and fellows can participate.

University College, which lays claim to be the earliest foundation, preserves in daily use an opening grace which combines elements of the original texts for *ante cibum* and *post cibum*. Its antiphonal first part is now followed by the usual prayers for Founder and benefactors. A similar exchange has taken place at Exeter for use on Sundays. Otherwise it is through feasts, patronal and commemorative, and gaudies that the use of the second grace is preserved. At feasts in Trinity in Cambridge, which is unique in having two High Tables, the usual grace before meat is said antiphonally by the Master and the Vice-Master; at the end of the meal the Chaplain and the choir similarly chant part of the postprandial grace.

While festal graces, both *ante* and *post cibum*, are a regular feature in the colleges of both universities with choral foundations of national reputation, where traditional settings are usually sung or chanted, it is encouraging to note that four-part choirs in other colleges are beginning to follow suit, sometimes with composition of new music. This not only enhances festal occasions, but helps to support the role of the Muse in university life.

Another alliterative two-word formula – *Benedicto benedicatur* has become a popular conclusion to dinner at High Table both in Cambridge and in Oxford. Its origin, like that of its pre-prandial equivalent, is obscure. It seems unlikely that such brief words of consecration would ever have been used in monasteries. The Benedictine Order makes no proprietorial claim to words which were not uncommon in pagan as well as in general use in Christian Latin. A revealing, if unkind, story is told by a Swiss Protestant writer at the end of the sixteenth century about an unlearned monk in a house of the Cistercian Order dedicated to St Bernard who coined the words which he thought corresponded – *Bernardus bernardat*.[14] This indicates that the original pairing was in frequent use at the time, perhaps as a monastic salutation in the cloister where brief communication was permitted. But no similar evidence has so far been found to suggest a correspondingly early date in respect of *Benedicto benedicatur*. This may, despite the impression of antiquity conveyed by the use of the verb in its impersonal form, yet prove to be an ingenious Victorian invention to provide a counterpart for use after dinner. If so, the identity of the composer is a well-kept secret.

That both pairings were in use as graces in Oxford by the middle of the nineteenth century is confirmed in a novel about undergraduate life at that period.[15] But 'Mr Verdant Green' con-fuses the issue by thinking that he heard after dinner *Benedicto benedicamur*. Agreement is now unlikely to be reached regarding the grammatical case of *Benedicto*. Should it be construed as dative or ablative? Suggested alternatives in translation will be found on page 82. Either would seem appropriate for this elegant and memorable benediction.

THE GRACES

T HE TEXTS for both universities were included in a com-
pendium of graces published in 1903, which incorporated a
record of those current in Oxford in 1857.[16] From these sources it
has been possible to reproduce in this collection some graces which
have not been heard in living memory. But while there is evidence
of disuse, there is proof of continuity in the wording of graces.

Although there are many texts *sui generis*, there is also a considerable amount of material held in common, but with a number
of textual variations. Colleges retain, however, a preference for
their own versions. Nevertheless the points of resemblance suggest
that the movement of doctors between colleges within the two
universities and the migration of some to foundations of colleges and schools elsewhere resulted in the transfer of popular
texts. The Caroline statutes of Trinity College, Dublin (1591),
for example, include the instructions, which are still followed,
to use at meal times wording familiar in the reign of Queen
Elizabeth. Its *ante cibum* grace is, in fact, a combination of the
corresponding graces at the colleges dedicated to the Trinity in
Cambridge (p. 49, first two lines) and at Oxford (p. 55).

The translations are in Prayer Book style throughout. It is
hoped that a literal interpretation in most cases will help those
unfamiliar with Latin to see without difficulty how the words
in English on the facing page of the graces of their own colleges
correspond with those in the texts.

The graces have been arranged in an approximate chronological
order of the dates of foundations, covering a span of seven and a
half centuries. The compositions of the present century are followed by a list of the colleges which use a two-word blessing.

A concluding Hebrew *Amen* can, of course, be said at the end
of a grace by all present, but the response has not been appended
to any of the texts.

Grace in the College of the Great Hall of the University
to be said each day before dinner.

May the Lord be blessed in his gifts
and holy in all his works.

Our help is in the name of the Lord,
who hath made heaven and earth.

May the name of the Lord be blessed
from this time forth and for evermore.

Lord God, the resurrection and the life of those who believe,
who art always to be praised both by the living and by the
dead, we give thee thanks for all our Founders and other
benefactors, by whose benefits we are here brought up in
godliness and learning: beseeching thee that, using these thy
gifts rightly to thy glory, we may with them be brought to
life immortal, through Jesus Christ our Lord.

May God grant grace to the living and repose to the dead:
peace and concord to the Church, to the Queen and our
kingdom: and to us sinners eternal life.

The title is reproduced from the card in use at the college.

UNIVERSITY COLLEGE
OXFORD (1249)

Gratiarum Actio in Collegio Magnae Aulae Universitatis
quotidie ante mensam dicenda.

Ante cibum

SCHOLAR Benedictus sit Deus in donis suis.
RESPONSE Et sanctus in omnibus operibus suis.

SCHOLAR Adjutorium nostrum in nomine Domini.
RESPONSE Qui fecit coelum et terras.

SCHOLAR Sit nomen Domini benedictum.
RESPONSE Ab hoc tempore usque in saecula.[17]

SCHOLAR Domine Deus, resurrectio et vita credentium,
qui semper es laudandus tam in viventibus quam
in defunctis, gratias tibi agimus pro omnibus
Fundatoribus caeterisque benefactoribus nostris,
quorum beneficiis hic ad pietatem et ad studia
literarum alimur: te rogantes ut nos, hisce tuis
donis ad tuam gloriam recte utentes, una cum iis
ad vitam immortalem perducamur, per Jesum
Christum Dominum nostrum.

Deus det vivis gratiam, defunctis requiem:
Ecclesiae, Reginae, regnoque nostro, pacem et
concordiam: et nobis peccatoribus vitam aeternam.

Blessed is God in his gifts
and holy in all his works.

Our help is in the name of the Lord
who hath made heaven and earth.

May the name of God be blessed
from this time forth for evermore.

Vouchsafe, Lord God, to bestow eternal life on all of us if we do
that which is good, for the sake of thy holy name.

The just man shall be held in eternal memory
and he shall nothing fear from evil report.

The souls of the righteous are in the hands of God
so that no means of wickedness should touch them.

Pour, we beseech thee, Lord God, thy grace into our minds so
that, using fitly and to thy glory these thy gifts made through
John Balliol and Dervorguilla, his wife, and all our other
benefactors, we may rise again to life in heaven with all the
faithful, through Jesus Christ our Lord.

May God of his infinite mercy bring unity and concord to
the Church, preserve the Queen and grant peace to this
kingdom and the Christian people, through Jesus Christ
our Lord.

BALLIOL
OXFORD (1263)

Post cibum

Benedictus est Deus in donis suis.
RESPONSE Et sanctus in omnibus operibus suis.

Adjutorium nostrum in nomine Domini est.
RESPONSE Qui fecit coelum et terras.

Sit nomen Dei benedictum.
RESPONSE Ab hoc tempore usque ad saecula.

Tribuere digneris, Domine Deus, nobis omnibus bona
facientibus ob tuum sanctum nomen vitam aeternam.

In memoria aeterna erit justus.
RESPONSE Et ab auditione mala nunquam timebit.

Justorum animae in manibus Dei sunt.
RESPONSE Ne tangant eos instrumenta nequitiae.

Funde, quaesumus, Domine Deus, in mentes nostras gratiam
tuam, ut tuis hisce donis datis a Johanne Balliolo et
Dervorguilla uxore, caeterisque omnibus benefactoribus nostris,
rite in tuam gloriam utentes in vitam una cum fidelibus
omnibus resurgamus, per Jesum Christum Dominum nostrum.

Deus pro infinita sua clementia Ecclesiae unitatem et
concordiam concedat, Reginam conservet, pacemque huic
regno populoque Christiano largiatur, per Jesum Christum
Dominum nostrum.

The eyes of all wait upon thee, O Lord.
Thou givest to them meat in due season.
Thou openest thine hand and fillest every living thing with thy
  blessing.
Bless for us, O Lord, all the gifts which of thy bounty we are
  about to partake, through Jesus Christ our Lord.

Because thou hast plentifully restored our bodies, O God, with
food and drink, and for thy kindness, we give thee the most
hearty thanks; and likewise we beseech thee to feed our minds
henceforth with thy word and spirit, so that eschewing all ills
we may perfectly understand and diligently consider those
things which will be pleasing to thy majesty, and that we may
make every effort to fulfil them, through Jesus Christ our Lord.

*The grace given here has not been used within the memory of current
fellows. What is now said after dinner is: Benedicto benedicatur.*

Bless us, O Lord, and thy gifts, which of thy bounty we are
about to receive, and grant that, being by them healthfully
nourished, we may be enabled to show our bounden duty
toward thee, through Christ our Lord.
  God is love, and he that dwelleth in love dwelleth in God
and God in him. May God be in us and may we dwell in him.

MERTON

Ante cibum

Oculi omnium in te respiciunt, Domine.
Tu das escam illis tempore opportuno.
Aperis manum tuam, et imples omne animal benedictione tua.[18]
Benedicas nobis, Domine, omnibus donis quae de tua
  beneficentia accepturi simus, per Jesum Christum
  Dominum nostrum.

Post cibum

Quod corpora nostra, Deus, cibo potuque abunde refecisti,
agimus tibi gratias, et benignitati tuae quantum possumus
maximas, simulque precamur ut animas nostras verbo spirituque
tuo deinceps pascas, ut mala omnia fugientes, ea quae placitura
sunt majestati tuae perfecte intelligamus, diligenterque
meditemur, et ad ea praestanda toto impetu feramur, per
Jesum Christum Dominum nostrum.

PETERHOUSE

CAMBRIDGE (1284)

Ante cibum

Benedic nos, Domine, et dona tua, quae de tua largitate
sumus sumpturi,[19] et concede ut illis salubriter nutriti tibi
debitum obsequium praestare valeamus, per Christum
Dominum nostrum.

  Deus est caritas, et qui manet in caritate in Deo manet,
et Deus in eo: sit Deus in nobis et nos maneamus in ipso.[20]

We give thee thanks, almighty and eternal God, for these and all thy benefits. Preserve, we beseech thee, the Catholic Church, the kingdom of Britain, Queen Elizabeth, and grant us eternal peace in Christ.

Blessed God, who feedest us from our youth, and providest food to all flesh, fill our hearts with joy and gladness, that we, having enough to satisfy us, may abound in every good work, through Jesus Christ our Lord, to whom, with thee and the Holy Spirit, be all honour, praise and power for all ages.

Lord God, the resurrection and life of all who believe in thee, who art always worthy to be praised by both the living and the dead, we give thee thanks for Edward the Second, our Founder, for Adam de Brome, our principal benefactor and for all our other benefactors, by whose benefits we are here maintained in godliness and learning; and we beseech thee that using these thy gifts rightly we may together be led to the immortal glory of resurrection, through Jesus Christ our Lord.

EXETER

OXFORD (1314)

Ante cibum (festal)

Gratias tibi agimus, omnipotens et aeterne Deus, pro his
atque omnibus beneficiis tuis. Conserves, quaesumus, Ecclesiam
Catholicam, regnum Britannicum, Reginam Elizabetham,
desque nobis pacem in Christo aeternam.

ORIEL

OXFORD (1326)

Ante cibum

Benedicte Deus, qui pascis nos a juventute nostra et praebes
cibum omni carni, reple gaudio et laetitia corda nostra ut nos
affatim quod satis est habentes abundemus in omne opus bonum,
per Jesum Christum Dominum nostrum, cui tecum et Spiritu
Sancto sit omnis honos, laus et imperium in saecula
saeculorum.[21]

Post cibum

Domine Deus, resurrectio et vita credentium, qui semper es
laudandus tum in viventibus tum in defunctis, agimus tibi
gratias pro Eduardo secundo, Fundatore nostro, pro Adamo de
Brome, praecipuo benefactore caeterisque benefactoribus nostris,
quorum beneficiis hic ad pietatem et ad studia bonarum
literarum alimur; rogantes ut nos his donis tuis recte utentes,
una cum illis, ad resurrectionis gloriam immortalem
perducamur, per Jesum Christum Dominum nostrum.

The eyes of all wait upon thee, O Lord;
Thou givest them their meat in due season.
Thou openest thine hand
And fillest every living thing with blessing.
Sanctify us, we beseech thee, O Lord, through thy word and prayer,
And consecrate these thy gifts, which through thy generosity
  we are about to receive,
Through Christ our Lord.

To thee be praise, honour and glory, for ever and ever,
O blessed and glorious Trinity.
Blessed be the name of the Lord.
We thank thee, omnipotent and eternal God
Who didst create all things by thy great power,
And by thy inscrutable wisdom dost govern the universe,
And by thy inexhaustible goodness dost feed and support every living
  creature.
We praise thee, most gracious Father,
For the most honoured Lady Elizabeth de Clare, our Foundress,
  and for all our other benefactors,
By whose gifts we are here nourished in godliness and learning,
Beseeching thee that, using these thy gifts aright and to thy glory
  in this age,
We together with the faithful may happily enjoy the world to come
  with thee, and that thou wilt bestow peace on all nations,
Through Christ our Lord.

May God in his infinite mercy
Grant concord and unity to his Church;
May he preserve our Queen and royal family;
May he give peace to all the world and all Christian people,
Through Christ our Lord.

CLARE
CAMBRIDGE (1326)

Ante cibum

Oculi omnium in te sperant Domine;
Tu das iis escam eorum in tempore opportuno.
Aperis tu manum tuam,
Et imples omne animal benedictione tua.
Sanctifica nos, quaesumus, Domine, per verbum et orationem,
Istisque tuis donis, quae de tua bonitate sumus accepturi,
    benedicito
Per Christum Dominum nostrum.

Post cibum

Tibi laus, tibi honos, tibi gloria, in saecula sempiterna,
O beata et gloriosa Trinitas.
Sit nomen Domini benedictum.
Gratias tibi agimus, omnipotens et sempiterne Deus
Qui tua ineffabili potentia condidisti omnia,
Tua inscrutabili sapientia gubernas universa,
Tua inexhausta bonitate cuncta pascis et vegetas.
Laudamus te, benignissime Pater,
Pro illustrissima Domina Elizabetha Domina de Clare,
    fundatrice nostra, caeterisque benefactoribus nostris,
Quorum beneficiis hic ad pietatem et studia literarum alimur;
Supplicantes tibi ut, hisce tuis donis recte in hoc saeculo ad
    tuam gloriam utentes,
Te una cum fidelibus in futuro feliciter perfruamur,
Tuque pacem omnibus terrarum gentibus elargiare,
Per Christum Dominum nostrum.

Deus pro infinita sua clementia
Ecclesiae suae concordiam et unitatem concedat;
Reginam nostram regiamque prosapiam conservet;
Pacem universo regno atque omnibus Christianis elargiatur,
Per Christum Dominum nostrum.

Bless us, Lord God, and these gifts, which of thy bounty we are about to receive, through Jesus Christ our Lord.

Blessed be God in his gifts
and hallowed in his works.

Our help is in the name of the Lord
who hath made heaven and earth.

May the name of the Lord be blessed
now and for evermore.

Vouchsafe, Lord God, to bestow eternal life on us all when we call upon thee in the holiness of thy name.

Lord God, the resurrection and the life of all who believe in thee, who art always to be praised both by the living and by the dead, we give thanks for our Founder, Robert Eglesfield, and our other benefactors, by whose charity we are here nursed in godliness and learning; and we beseech thee that, using these gifts rightly to the glory of thy name, we may be translated to the everlasting glory of the resurrection, through Jesus Christ our Lord.

May God grant grace to the living, rest to the departed, peace and concord to the Church, the Queen and our realm and to us sinners eternal life.

THE QUEEN'S
OXFORD (1341)

Ante cibum

Benedic nobis, Domine Deus, et his donis, quae ex liberalitate tua sumpturi sumus, per Jesum Christum Dominum nostrum.

Post cibum

VERSICLE	Benedictus sit Deus in donis suis.
RESPONSE	Sanctus et in operibus suis.
VERSICLE	Adjutorium nostrum in nomine Domini.
RESPONSE	Qui fecit coelum et terras.
VERSICLE	Sit nomen Domini benedictum.
RESPONSE	Nunc, usque et in saecula.

Dignere, Domine Deus, largiri nobis omnibus te invocantibus propter nomen tuum sanctum vitam aeternam.

Domine Deus, resurrectio et vita credentium, qui semper es laudandus tum in viventibus, tum in defunctis, agimus tibi gratias pro Fundatore nostro Roberto Eglesfield, caeterisque nostris benefactoribus, quorum beneficiis hic ad pietatem et literarum studia alimur; rogantes te ut nos, his donis recte utentes in nominis tui gloriam, ad resurrectionis gloriam perpetuam perducamur, per Jesum Christum Dominum nostrum.

Deus det vivis gratiam, defunctis requiem, Ecclesiae, Reginae, regnoque nostro pacem et concordiam et nobis peccatoribus vitam aeternam.

We give thee thanks, O God and Father, for so many favours, which thou dost continually bestow upon us, and for thy unbounden generosity, through Jesus Christ our Lord.

Bless, O Lord, thy gifts to our use and us to thy service, through Jesus Christ our Lord.

Whatever is or whatever shall be placed before us, may God bless these his gifts to our use, and ourselves to his service, through Jesus Christ our Lord.

ST EDMUND HALL

OXFORD (*c.*1278)[22]

Post cibum

Agimus tibi gratias, Deus et Pater, pro tot beneficiis,
quae nobis assidue et pro infinita tua liberalitate largiris,
per Jesum Christum Dominum nostrum.

PEMBROKE

CAMBRIDGE (1347)

Ante cibum

Benedic, Domine, dona tua in usum nostrum et nos in servitium
tuum, per Jesum Christum Dominum nostrum.

or

Quidquid nobis appositum est, aut quidquid apponetur,
benedicat Deus haec sua dona in usum nostrum, necnon nosmet
ipsos in servitium suum, per Jesum Christum Dominum
nostrum.[23]

Bless, O Lord, us and thy gifts which, of thy bounty we are about to receive, and grant that, being by them wholesomely fed, we may be able to render that worship which is thy due, through Jesus Christ our Lord. Make us partakers of the heavenly table, O King of everlasting glory.

Let us give thanks to God for our beloved college;
and for all our benefactors.

Remembrance of the righteous will endure for ever;
nor shall he ever fear the tongues of men that speak evil,

The Lord be with you,
and with thy spirit.

We give thanks, almighty God, who livest and reignest for ever, for all thy blessings, for our Founders, Edmund Gonville, William Bateman and John Caius and for all our benefactors.

May God grant concord and unity to his Church, preserve Elizabeth our Queen and the royal family, and bring peace to the whole kingdom and all Christian people.

The eyes of all hope in you, O Lord: and you grant their food in due season. Glory to you, O Lord.

With the fruit of your works the earth is filled: so that you bring forth bread from the earth. And wine cheers the hearts of all: so that oil gladdens their faces and bread strengthens their hearts. Thanks be to God.

Ante cibum

Benedic, Domine, nobis et donis tuis, quae ex largitate tua
sumus sumpturi, et concede ut, ab iis salubriter enutriti, tibi
debitum obsequium praestare valeamus, per Jesum Christum
Dominum nostrum. Mensae coelestis nos participes facias,
Rex aeternae gloriae.[24]

Post cibum

VERSICLE   Gratias Deo agamus pro collegio dilectissimo;
RESPONSE   Et pro omnibus benefactoribus nostris.

VERSICLE   Memoria justorum in sempiternum durabit;
RESPONSE   Nec metuet unquam maledicentium rumores.

VERSICLE   Dominus vobiscum.
RESPONSE   Et cum spiritu tuo.

Agimus tibi gratias, omnipotens Deus, pro omnibus beneficiis
tuis, pro Fundatoribus nostris Edmundo Gonville, Gulielmo
Bateman et Iohanne Caio, et pro omnibus benefactoribus
nostris, qui vivis et regnas Deus per omnia secula.

    Deus Ecclesiae suae concordiam et unitatem concedat,
Elizabetham Reginam nostram regiamque prosapiam conservet,
et pacem regno universo atque omnibus Christianis largiatur.

Benedictio ante mensam

Oculi omnium in te sperant, Domine: et tu das escam illorum
in tempore opportuno. Gloria tibi Domine.

Gratia post mensam

De fructu operum tuorum satiabitur terra: ut educas panem
de terra. Et vinum laetificet cor hominis: ut exhilaret faciem in
oleo, et panis cor hominis confirmet. Deo gratias.

Whatever is before us or shall be placed before us, let Christ be pleased to bless in the name of the Father and of the Son and of the Holy Spirit.

Bless us, O Lord, and thy gifts, which of thy bounty we are about to receive, through Jesus Christ our Lord.
Make us share in thy heavenly table, O King of everlasting glory.
God is love, and he that dwelleth in love dwelleth in God, and God in him. May God be in us, and may we dwell in him.

> We bless the Lord.
> Thanks be to God.

We give thee thanks, almighty and eternal God, for all thy blessings, who livest and reignest God over all, world without end.
May God preserve the Church, the Queen, and all the royal family, and the realm; may he grant us peace, and after death life eternal.

May the King of eternal glory make us partakers of the heavenly table.
Bless, O Lord, us and thy gifts, which of thy bounty we are about to receive; and grant that being by them wholesomely fed we may be enabled to show our bounden duty toward thee, through Christ our Lord.

> Praise be to God through our Lord Jesus Christ.
> Thanks be to God.

TRINITY HALL
CAMBRIDGE (1350)

Ante cibum (ferial)

Quicquid appositum est aut apponetur Christus benedicere
dignetur, in nomine Patris et Filii et Spiritus Sancti.

Ante cibum (festal)

Benedic nobis, Domine, et donis tuis, quae de largitate tua
    sumpturi sumus, per Jesum Christum Dominum nostrum.
Mensae caelestis participes nos facias, Rex aeternae gloriae.
Deus est caritas, et qui manet in caritate manet in Deo,
    et Deus in eo. Sit Deus in nobis, et nos maneamus in illo.

Post cibum (festal)

VERSICLE   Benedicimus Domino.
RESPONSE   Deo gratias.

Agimus tibi gratias, omnipotens et sempiterne Deus, pro omnibus
tuis beneficiis, qui vivis et regnas Deus per omnia, in saecula
saeculorum.

    Deus servet Ecclesiam, et Reginam, totamque regiam
familiam, et regnum; det nobis pacem, et post mortem
vitam aeternam.

CORPUS CHRISTI
CAMBRIDGE (1352)

Ante cibum

Mensae caelestis participes faciat nos Rex gloriae aeternae.
    Benedic, Domine, nobis et donis tuis, quae de tua largitate
sumus sumpturi; et concede ut iis salubriter nutriti tibi debitum
obsequium praestare valeamus, per Christum Dominum nostrum.

Post cibum

VERSICLE   Laus Deo per Jesum Christum Dominum nostrum.
RESPONSE   Deo gratias.

The first grace below is used on 'Election day' of scholars from Winchester College, which is part of the double foundation of William of Wykeham.

We give thee thanks almighty Lord for our Founder, William of Wykeham, and for the others by whose benefits we are here brought up to godliness and learning; beseeching thee that we, using these thy gifts to the honour of thy name, may pass on to the immortal glory of thy resurrection, through Jesus Christ our Lord.

The eyes of all wait upon thee, O Lord. Thou givest them meat in due season. Thou openest thine hand and fillest every living thing with thy blessing.

May the Lord be blessed in his gifts and holy in all his works. Our help is in the name of the Lord who made heaven and earth. May the name of the Lord be blessed from this time forth for evermore. Bless ye the Lord.

Make us partakers of the heavenly table, O King of eternal glory.

NEW COLLEGE
OXFORD (1379)

When the hall was restored in 1865, heraldic glass was designed for its seven windows. In a border above and beneath is a running sequence of the text of graces visible in daylight.

Agimus tibi gratias omnipotens Deus pro fundatore nostro, Gulielmo de Wykeham, reliquisque quorum beneficiis hic ad pietatem et ad studia literarum alimur; rogantes ut nos, his donis tuis ad nominis tui honorem recte utentes, ad resurrectionis tuae gloriam perducamur immortalem, per Jesus Christum Dominum nostrum.

Oculi omnium spectant in te, Domine. Tu das iis escam in tempore opportuno. Tu aperis manum tuam et imples omnium animal benediction tua.

Benedictus sit Deus in donis suis et sanctus in omnibus operibus eius. Adjutorium nostrum est in nomine Domini qui fecit coelum et terram. Sit nomen Domini benedictum ex hoc nunc usque in saeculum. Benedicite Domino.

Mensae coelestis participes nos facias, Rex aeternae gloriae.

Most gracious Father, who governest with thy providence, feedest with thy goodness and preservest with thy blessing all things which thou shalt have created, bless us, we beseech thee and these thy creatures for our use that they may be hallowed and healthy for us and that we, thereby strengthened, may be the readier for all good works in praise of thy eternal name, through Jesus Christ our Lord.

Eternal God, giver of all good things, we give thee thanks for our election, redemption, preservation and today for this resuscitation; and also for Richard Fleming and Thomas Rotheram, our Founders, and for all benefactors else whom it has pleased thee so to move that they did provide these outstanding gifts for us. We pray and beseech thee that their generosity, which is honoured in continued memory, may encourage many others to emulate that same goodness, and we pray that mindful of them day by day we may not be found unworthy of such great blessings, through Jesus Christ our Lord.

May God of his unbounded goodness preserve, protect and defend the Church worldwide, our Queen and all this realm, strengthen our faith, forgive our sins, bring comfort to the afflicted and restore to us peace everlasting in Christ.

LINCOLN
OXFORD (1427)

Ante cibum

Benignissime Pater, qui providentia tua regis, liberalitate pascis
et benedictione conservas omnia quae creaveris, benedicas nobis
te quaesumus et hisce creaturis in usum nostrum ut illae
sanctificatae sint et nobis salutares, et ut nos inde corroborati
magis apti reddamur ad omnia opera bona, in laudem tui
nominis aeterni, per Jesum Christum Dominum nostrum.

Post cibum

Aeterne Deus, bonorum omnium largitor, agimus tibi gratias
pro electione, redemptione, conservatione, praesentique hac
refocillatione; atque etiam pro Ricardo Fleming et Thoma
Rotheram, Fundatoribus nostris, caeterisque benefactoribus quos
excitare dignatus es ad eximia bona nobis praeparanda; supplices
te orantes ut eorum beneficia, quae ad sempiternam donatorum
memoriam vigent, complures alios ad eandem pietatem
aemulandam excitare possint, et eorum quotidie memores non
indigni reperiamur hac tanta benedictione, per Jesum Christum
Dominum nostrum.

Ecclesiam universam, Reginam, totum hoc regnum Deus pro
immensa sua bonitate conservet, protegat et defendat, fidem
nostram adaugeat, peccata remittat, afflictis solatium afferat,
et pacem in Christo nobis sempiternam reddat.

May God, the Father and the Son and the Holy Spirit, bless what is before us and what is to follow.

Thanks be to God, the Father and the Son and the Holy Spirit.

Bless, O Lord, us and these thy gifts, which from thy grace and bounty we are about to receive; and grant that being through them healthfully nourished by thee we may be enabled to show our bounden duty toward thee, through Christ our Lord.

The eyes of all wait upon thee, O Lord, and thou providest their meat in due season. Glory be to thee, O Lord.

ALL SOULS
OXFORD (1438)

Ante cibum

Appositis et apponendis benedicat Deus, Pater et Filius
et Spiritus Sanctus.

Post cibum

Benedicatur Deo, Patri et Filio et Spiritui Sancto.

KING'S
CAMBRIDGE (1441)

IN PRESENT USE

Ante cibum (*ferial*)

Benedic, Domine, nobis et his donis tuis, quae de tua gratia
et munificentia sumus iam sumpturi; et concede ut, illis
salubriter a te nutriti, tibi debitum obsequium praestare
valeamus, per Christum Dominum nostrum.

Ante cibum (*festal – sung*)

Oculi omnium in te sperant, Domine, et tu das escam illorum
in tempore opportuno. Gloria tibi, Domine.

Bless ye
the Lord.

The eyes of all wait upon thee, O Lord,
and thou givest them their meat in due season.

Thou openest thine hand
and fillest every living thing with blessing.

Glory be to the Father and to the Son and to the Holy Spirit,
as it was in the beginning, is now and ever shall be.

Bless, O Lord, us and these thy gifts, which of thy grace and
generosity we are about to receive.

God is love; he who abideth in love abideth in God and God
in him. Let God abide in us and let us abide in him.

Pour, we beseech thee, O Lord, thy grace into our hearts that
rightly using these gifts of King Henry VI our Founder to thy
glory we together with all the faithful departed may rise again
to heavenly life, through Christ our Lord.

Lord have mercy. Christ have mercy. Lord have mercy.

*Then shall be sung by a choir an antiphon of the choice of the Vice-Provost
such as shall be suitable for the occasion. Which ended there shall be said:*

May Christ, the Son of Mary, be merciful and kind unto us;
may he guide his Church; may he preserve the Queen and the
realm, and keep us safe in Christian peace.

KING'S

IN PAST USE

Ante cibum

VERSICLE	Benedicite
RESPONSE	Domino.
VERSICLE	Oculi omnium sperant in te Domine
RESPONSE	Et tu das escam illorum in tempore.
VERSICLE	Aperis manum tuam
RESPONSE	Et imples omne animal benedictione.
VERSICLE	Gloria Patri et Filio et Spiritui Sancto
RESPONSE	Sicut erat in principio et nunc et in saecula saeculorum.

Benedic, Domine, nobis et his donis tuis quae de tua gratia et munificentia sumus sumpturi.

    LECTIO   Deus caritas est; qui manet in caritate in Deo manet, et Deus in eo. Sit Deus in nobis et nos maneamus in ipso.

Post cibum

Infunde, quaesumus, Domine Deus, gratiam in mentes nostras ut his donis datis ab Henrico Sexto Rege Fundatore nostro recte ad tuam gloriam utentes una tandem cum fidelibus defunctis omnibus ad caelestem vitam resurgamus per Christum Dominum nostrum.

Kyrie Eleison. Christe Eleison. Kyrie Eleison.

Tunc cantetur a choro aliquo antiphona ad placitum Vice-praepositi quae magis tempori conveniat. Qua finita dicitur:

Christus, Mariae filius, sit nobis clemens et propitius; gubernet suam Ecclesiam; conservet Reginam et regnum; et nos tuetur in Christiana pace.

Bless, O Lord, us and thy gifts, which from thy bounty we are about to receive, and grant that being by them healthfully nourished we may be enabled to show our bounden duty toward thee, through Christ our Lord.

We give thee thanks, eternal God, because thou hast vouchsafed to feed us so generously at this time, and we bless thy holy name for the Queens, our Foundresses, and for other benefactors, through whose benevolence we are here brought up in godliness and learning, and we beseech thee that we, using these gifts rightly to thy glory, together with those who have died in the faith of Christ, may continue into heavenly life, through Christ our Lord.

God preserve our Queen and the Church.

or

For these and all his mercies, for the Queens our Foundresses, and for our other benefactors, God's holy name be blessed and praised. God preserve our Queen and Church.

QUEENS'
CAMBRIDGE (1448)

Ante cibum

Benedic, Domine, nos et dona tua, quae de largitate tua
sumus sumpturi, et concede ut illis salubriter nutriti tibi
debitum obsequium praestare valeamus, per Christum
Dominum nostrum.

Post cibum

Gratias tibi agimus, sempiterne Deus, quod tarn benigne hoc
tempore nos pascere dignatus es, benedicentes sanctum nomen
tuum pro Reginis, Fundatricibus nostris, caeterisque
Benefactoribus, quorum beneficiis hic ad pietatem et studia
literarum alimur, petimusque ut nos, his donis ad tuam gloriam
recte utentes, una cum illis qui in fide Christi decesserunt, ad
coelestem vitam perducamur, per Christum Dominum nostrum.
Deus salvam fac Reginam atque Ecclesiam.

An abbreviated form of this is used for the post cibum grace in English

God of peace and love be pleased to abide with us, we beseech thee, and thou Lord, have mercy upon us.

All thy works praise thee, O Lord. All thy saints praise thee. Praise ye the Lord all nations. All his people praise ye the Lord. Because his mercy towards us is assured and the truth of the Lord remaineth for all time. Glory be to the Father and to the Son and to the Holy Spirit. As it was in the beginning, is now and ever shall be.

He has distributed gifts to the poor. His justice remaineth for ever and his horn shall be exalted in glory. I will always bless the Lord. His praise shall always be in my mouth. Sing unto the Lord and bless his name. Tell the nations of his glory and speak of his wonders to all people. Grant, merciful Father, to us miserable sinners eternal life for thy holy name's sake, through Jesus Christ our Lord.

This is followed by the Commemoration of the Departed

The righteous shall be held in everlasting remembrance; nor shall they fear any evil report. Their bodies are buried in peace, and their names shall live from one generation to another. Men shall tell of their wisdom and the Church will speak their praises.

O Lord God, the resurrection and life of all that trust in thee, who art always to be blessed for thy gifts and holy works, we give unending thanks to thy majesty for William Waynfleet, our Founder, and for all our benefactors and for the many blessings which thou hast delivered unto us through their hands; and we humbly beseech thee that we may use these thy gifts aright to the honour of thy name and together with thine elect be made partakers of thy eternal glory in the kingdom of heaven, through Jesus Christ our Lord.

MAGDALEN

Ante cibum (festal)

Deus pacis et caritatis digneris quaesumus habitare nobiscum, et tu Domine miserere nostrum.

Laudant te omnia opera tua, Domine. Laudant te omnes sancti tui. Laudate Dominum omnes gentes. Laudate eum omnes populi ejus. Quoniam confirmata est supra nos misericordia ejus et veritas Domini manet in aeternum. Gloria sit Patri et Filio et Spiritui Sancto. Sicut erat in principio, sic nunc est et erit in saecula saeculorum.

Dispersit et dedit pauperibus. Et justitia ejus manet in saeculum saeculi et cornu ejus exaltabitur in gloria. Semper benedicam Domino. Semper in ore meo laus ejus. Cantate Domino et benedicite nomini ejus. Enunciate inter gentes gloriam ejus, in omnibus populis admirabilia ejus. Largire nobis, misericors Pater, miserrimis peccatoribus aeternam vitam propter nomen sanctum tuum, per Jesum Christum Dominum nostrum.

In memoria aeterna erunt justi; ab auditione mala non timebunt. Corpora eorum in pace sepulta sunt, et nomina eorum vivant a generatione in generationem. Sapientiam eorum narrabunt populi et laudes eorum enunciabit Ecclesia.

Domine Deus, resurrectio et vita eorum omnium qui in te confidunt, qui semper benedictus es in donis tuis et sanctis in operibus, immortales gratias agimus majestati tuae pro Gulielmo de Waynflete, Fundatore nostro, et pro omnibus benefactoribus nostris, amplissimisque beneficiis tuis, quae nobis per manus eorum tradidisti; teque suppliciter obsecramus ut nos hisce donis tuis recte utamur ad nominis tui honorem, ut una cum sanctis tuis aeternae gloriae in coelis participes fiamus, per Jesum Christum Dominum nostrum.

Thanksgiving Hymn

Thee, mighty Father, we adore,
and praise thy Name for evermore,
whose bounty feeds all Adam's race,
and cheers the hungry soul with grace.

Great co-eternal Son, to thee
with one consent we bow the knee,
for our salvation man become,
thou didst not scorn the virgin's womb.

The Paschal Lamb, foreshown of old,
in thee, sweet Jesus, we behold,
and pardon through thy blood receive,
while on thy cross we look and live.

Thee too, all hallowed mystic Dove,
we ever bless and ever love;
thy wonders how shall we declare,
the Lord was born, the virgin bare.

Almighty everlasting three,
no other God we have but thee,
thy glorious work, immortal King
in triumph thus we daily sing.

This translation of what he called a 'Monkish Latin Hymn' was made by the Rt Revd George Horne, who in 1750 was elected a Fellow of the College, of which he was to become President in 1768. It became a fashionable hymn of praise in the style of his contemporaries Isaac Watts and Charles Wesley.

MAGDALEN

OXFORD

Hymnus Eucharisticus

Te Deum Patrem colimus,
te laudibus prosequimur,
qui corpus cibo reficis,
caelesti mentem gratia.

Te adoramus, O Jesu,
te, Fili unigenite,
te, qui non dedignatus es
subire claustra Virginis.

Actus in crucem factus es
irato Deo victima:
per te, Salvator unice,
vitae spes nobis rediit.

Tibi, aeterne Spiritus,
cujus afflatu peperit
infantem Deum Maria
aeternum benedicimus.

Triune Deus, hominum
salutis Auctor optime,
immensum hoc mysterium
ovante lingua canimus.

These verses were written by a Fellow of Magdalen, Thomas Smith, as a College grace, and set to music by Benjamin Rogers during his period as organist between 1665 and 1686. It came into use as the May morning music sung from the Great Tower probably about a century later. The hymn is now sung at feasts after an abbreviated version of the text in the last paragraph of p. 31.

The eyes of all look toward and trust in thee, O Lord.
Thou givest them their meats in due season.
Thou openest thine hands and fillest all living things
    with thy blessing.
Bless us, O Lord, and all thy gifts,
    which of thy great bounty we are about to receive,
    through our Lord Jesus Christ.

May the Lord be blessed in his gifts.
Our help is in the name of the Lord, who made heaven
    and earth.
May the name of the Lord be blessed.
We give thanks, Almighty God,
    for our Founder and other benefactors,
    and for all thy benefits,
    who livest and reignest, God for ever and ever.
May God guard the Church, the Queen, the princes,
    the kingdom, truth and peace.

ST CATHARINE'S
CAMBRIDGE (1473)

Ante cibum

Oculi omnium aspiciunt et in te sperant, Domine.
Tu das iis escas illorum tempore opportuno.
Aperis tu manus et imples omne animal benedictione tua.
Benedic nobis, Domine, et omnibus donis tuis,
 quae ex larga liberalitate tua sumpturi sumus,
 per Dominum nostrum Jesum Christum.

Post cibum

Benedictus sit Dominus in donis suis.
Adjutorium nostrum in nomine Domini, qui fecit coelum
 et terram.
Sit nomen Domini benedictum.
Agimus tibi gratias, omnipotens Deus,
 pro Fundatore caeterisque benefactoribus nostris,
 et pro universis beneficiis tuis,
 qui vivis et regnas Deus in saecula saeculorum.
Deus conservet Ecclesiam, Reginam, principes, regnum,
 veritatem et pacem.

The eyes of all look towards thee and trust in thee, O God. Thou givest meat to them in due season. Thou openest thy hands and fillest every living thing with thy blessing.

Bless us, O Lord, and all thy gifts, which through thy great bounty we are about to receive, through Jesus Christ our Lord.

God is love. He who abideth in love abideth in God and God in him. Let God be in us and let us abide in him.

May the God of peace and love abide with us always; and do thou, O Lord, have mercy upon us.

We thank thee for all thy mercies, who livest and reignest, God, world without end.

May God preserve the Church, the Queen, the kingdom, Parliament and the peace.

Praise be to God.
Thanks be to God.

JESUS
CAMBRIDGE (1496)

Ante cibum

Oculi omnium in te aspiciunt et in te sperant, Deus. Tu das illis escam tempore opportuno. Aperis tu manus, et imples omne animal benedictione tua.

Benedic nobis, Domine, et omnibus tuis donis, quae ex larga liberalitate tua sumpturi sumus, per Jesum Christum Dominum nostrum.

Deus est caritas. Qui manet in caritate manet in Deo et Deus in illo. Sit Deus in nobis, et nos maneamus in illo.

Post cibum (*festal*)

Deus pacis et dilectionis semper maneat nobiscum; tu autem, Domine, miserere nostrum.

Agimus tibi gratias pro omnibus tuis beneficiis, qui vivis et regnas, Deus, per omnia saecula saeculorum.

Deus conservet Ecclesiam, Reginam, regnum, senatum, et pacem.

Post cibum (*ferial*)

Laus Deo.
Deo gratias.

The eyes of all look with hope towards thee, O Lord, and thou givest them meat in thy good time. Thou openest thine hand and fillest every living thing with blessing.

Whatever is, or shall be put before us, may he who feeds all with his bounty bid it to be wholesome and holy.

Our Father, which art in heaven, hallowed be thy name; thy kingdom come; thy will be done, on earth as it is in heaven. Give us this day our daily bread, and forgive us our trespasses as we forgive those who trespass against us. And lead us not into temptation, but deliver us from evil, for thine is the kingdom, the power and the glory, for ever and ever.

Lord all holy, Father all powerful, and eternal God, who art pleased to feed us at this time so kindly and generously, grant out of thy goodness towards us, that we may always give hearty thanks to thee, live honest and good lives and follow those studies which may show thy glory and support thy Church, through Christ our Lord.

May God of his infinite mercy grant concord and unity to his Church, preserve Elizabeth our Queen and the royal family and bestow peace on the whole kingdom and all Christian people.

CHRIST'S
CAMBRIDGE (1505)

Ante prandium

Oculi omnium in te sperant, Domine, et tu das escam illis in tempore suo. Aperis manum tuam, et imples omne animal benedictione.

Quicquid appositum est, aut apponetur, felix et sanctum esse jubeat, qui sua bonitate pascit universa.

Pater noster, qui es in caelis, sanctificetur nomen tuum, adveniat regnum tuum; fiat voluntas tua sicut in caelo, sic etiam in terra. Panem nostrum quotidianum da nobis hodie. Et remitte nobis debita nostra, sicut nos remittimus debitoribus nostris. Et ne nos inducas in tentationem, sed libera nos a malo, quia tuum est regnum, potentia et gloria in saecula saeculorum.[26]

Post prandium

Domine sancte, Pater omnipotens, et aeterne Deus, qui tam benigne et liberaliter hoc tempore pascere nos dignatus es; largire nobis, ut tibi semper, pro tua in nos bonitate, ex animo gratias agamus, vitam honeste et pie transigamus, et studia ea sectemur quae tuam gloriam illustrare et Ecclesiae adiumento esse possint, per Christum Dominum nostrum.

Deus, pro sua infinita clementia, Ecclesiae suae concordiam et unitatem concedat, Reginam nostram Elizabetham sobolemque regiam conservet et pacem universo regno et omnibus Christianis largiatur.

Christ, the gladdener of all, without whom nothing is sweet or pleasant, bless, we pray thee, the food and drink of thy servants, which thou hast now provided for our bodily sustenance; and grant that we may use these thy gifts to praise thee, and enjoy them with grateful hearts; grant also that, as our body is nurtured by bodily foods, so may our mind feed on the spiritual nourishment of thy word, through thee, our Lord.

Blessed be God in his gifts, and holy in his works. Let the name of the Lord be blessed, now and for evermore. Bless the Lord, O my soul, and let all that is within me bless his holy name.

Most merciful Father, who, moved not by our worth but by thy goodness alone, art pleased to refresh us this night so favourably and freely, speedily grant that we, filled with thy grace, may continually worship thee, speak thy praises, and in word and deed follow what is pleasing unto thee, through Christ our Lord.

May God, of his infinite mercy, grant concord and unity to his Church, preserve Elizabeth our Queen and the royal family and bestow peace on the whole kingdom and all Christian people.

CHRIST'S
CAMBRIDGE

Ante coenam

Exhilarator omnium Christe, sine quo nihil suave, nihil
jucundum est, benedic, quaesumus, cibo et potui servorum
tuorum, quae jam ad alimonium corporis apparavisti: et concede
ut istis muneribus tuis ad laudem tuam utamur, gratisque animis
fruamur; utque quemadmodum corpus nostrum cibis
corporalibus fovetur, ita mens nostra spirituali verbi tui
nutrimento pascatur, per te, Dominum nostrum.[27]

Post coenam

Benedictus Deus in donis suis, et sanctus in operibus suis. Sit
nomen Domini benedictum, et nunc et in seculum. Benedic,
anima mea, Domino, et omnia quae intra me sunt sancto
nomini ejus.

Clementissime Pater, qui, non nostris meritis sed tua sola
bonitate inductus, hac nocte tam benigne et liberaliter reficere
nos dignatus es, concede propitius ut, tua gratia repleti, te
assidue colamus, laudes tuas celebremus, et, quae tibi sunt
placita, dictis et factis exsequamur, per Christum Dominum
nostrum.

Deus, pro sua infinita clementia, Ecclesiae suae concordiam et
unitatem concedat, Reginam nostram Elizabetham sobolemque
regiam conservet, et pacem universo regno et omnibus
Christianis largiatur.

The eyes of all look to thee, O God. Thou givest them meats in due season. Thou openest thy hand and fillest every living thing with thy blessing.

Make us participants at the heavenly banquet, O God, King of eternal glory.

May he who hath created, redeemed and provided for us be blessed for ever. Hear our prayer, Lord. We give thee thanks, heavenly Father, for William Smyth, Bishop, and Richard Sutton, Knight, our Founders; for Alexander Nowel, Joyce Frankland, Elizabeth Morley, Maurice Platnauer and for our other benefactors, humbly beseeching thee that thou wilt add to their number in goodness.

Safeguard the Catholic Church and all Christian people. Root out all heretical waverings. Defend Elizabeth our Queen and her subjects. Grant peace and preserve it, through Christ our Lord.

Almighty and eternal God, without whom nothing is sweet, nothing bears odour, we humbly seek thy mercy to bless us and our meal and to gladden our hearts so that we may receive and dedicate to thy honour and loving kindness the food of which we are about to partake, through Christ our Lord.

Because thou hast plentifully restored our bodies, O great and mighty God, with food and drink, we give thee the most hearty thanks; and likewise we beseech thee to feed our minds henceforth with thy word and spirit, so that eschewing all ills we may perfectly understand and diligently consider those things which will be pleasing to thee, and may hasten to perform them, through Christ our Lord.

BRASENOSE

OXFORD (1509)[28]

Ante cibum (prandium)

Oculi omnium spectant in te, Deus. Tu das illis escas tempore opportuno. Aperis manum tuam et imples omne animal tua benedictione.

Mensae caelestis nos participes facias, Deus, Rex aeternae gloriae.

Post cibum (prandium)

Qui nos creavit, redemit et pavit, sit benedictus in aeternum. Deus, exaudi orationem nostram. Agimus tibi gratias, Pater caelestis, pro Gulielmo Smyth episcopo, et Ricardo Sutton milite, Fundatoribus nostris; pro Alexandro Nowel, Jocosa Frankland, Gulielmo Hulme, Elizabetha Morley, Mauritio Platnauer, aliisque benefactoribus nostris; humiliter te precantes ut eorum numerum benignissime adaugeas.

Ecclesiam Catholicam, et populum Christianum custodi. Haereses et errores omnes extirpa. Elizabetham Reginam nostram et subditos eius defende. Pacem da et conserva, per Christum Dominum nostrum.

Ante cibum (coenam)

Omnipotens et sempiterne Deus, sine quo nihil est dulce, nihil odoriferum, misericordiam tuam humiliter imploramus, ut nos coenamque nostram benedicas; ut corda nostra exhilares; ut quae suscepturi sumus alimenta, tuo honori, tuaeque beneficentiae accepta referamus, per Christum Dominum nostrum.

Post cibum (coenam)

Quod corpora nostra, Deus optime maxime, cibo potuque abunde refecisti, agimus tibi gratias, quantas possumus maximas; simulque precamur, ut animas nostras verbo et spiritu deinde pascas; ut omnia mala fugiamus; ut quae sint tibi placitura perfecte intelligamus, diligenter meditemur, et ad ea praestanda toto impetu feramur, per Christum Dominum nostrum.

The eyes of all creatures look to thee in hope, O Lord, and thou givest them food in due time, openest thine hand and fillest every creature with blessing.

Bless, O Lord, us and thy gifts, which of thy bounty we are about to receive, and grant that being by them wholesomely fed we may be enabled to show our bounden duty toward thee, through Jesus Christ our Lord.

Pour, we beseech thee, Lord God, thy grace into our hearts that we use these gifts of Margaret our Foundress and other benefactors to thy glory; and with all who have died in the faith of Christ may we rise to heavenly life, through Jesus Christ our Lord.

May God in his infinite mercy grant peace and unity to his Church, watch over our most illustrious Queen Elizabeth, and bestow his peace on the whole realm and on all Christian people.

ST JOHN'S
CAMBRIDGE (1511)

Ante cibum

Oculi omnium in te sperant, Domine, et tu das illis cibum in tempore, aperis manum tuam et imples omne animal benedictione.

Benedic, Domine, nos et dona tua, quae de tua largitate sumus sumpturi, et concede ut illis salubriter nutriti, tibi debitum obsequium praestare valeamus, per Jesum Christum Dominum nostrum.

Post cibum

Infunde, quaesumus, Domine Deus, gratiam tuam in mentes nostras, ut his donis datis a Margareta fundatrice nostra aliisque benefactoribus ad tuam gloriam utamur; et cum omnibus qui in fide Christi decesserunt ad caelestem vitam resurgamus, per Jesum Christum Dominum nostrum.

Deus pro sua infinita clementia ecclesiae suae pacem et unitatem concedat, augustissimam reginam nostram Elizabetham conservet, et pacem universo regno et omnibus Christianis largiatur.

At great feasts an anthem is sung between the two sections of the post cibum grace.

We wretched and needy men reverently give thee thanks, almighty God, heavenly Father, for this food which thou hast sanctified and bestowed for the sustenance of our body, so that we may use it aright. At the same time we beseech thee that thou wilt impart to us the food of angels, the true bread of heaven, the eternal word of God Jesus Christ our Lord, so that the mind of each of us may feed on him and that through his flesh and blood we may be nourished, sustained and strengthened.

Pour, we beseech thee, Lord God, thy grace into our hearts, that we, rightly using these thy gifts, made to us by Richard Fox, our Founder, and all other benefactors, to thy glory, may together with all the faithful departed rise again to life in heaven, through Jesus Christ our Lord.

May God of his infinite mercy grant concord and unity to his Church, preserve our Queen, bring peace to the whole realm and to Christian people, through Jesus Christ our Lord.

Bless, O Lord, us and thy gifts, which through thy bounty we are about to receive; and grant that being by them healthfully nourished, we may be enabled to show our bounden duty toward thee, through Jesus Christ our Lord and Saviour.

Praise be to God.
Thanks be to God.

CORPUS CHRISTI
OXFORD (1517)

Ante cibum

Nos miseri et egentes homines, pro hoc cibo quem in alimonium corporis nostri sanctificatum es largitus, ut eo recte utamur, tibi, Deus omnipotens, Pater caelestis, reverenter gratias agimus, simul obsecrantes ut cibum angelorum, panem verum caelestem, Dei verbum aeternum Jesum Christum Dominum nostrum nobis impertiaris, ut eo mens nostra pascatur, et per carnem et sanguinem ejus alamur, foveamur, corroboremur.

Post cibum

Infunde, quaesumus, Domine Deus, gratiam tuam in mentes nostras, ut hisce donis tuis, datis a Ricardo Fox, Fundatore nostro, caeterisque benefactoribus nostris, recte in tuam gloriam utentes, una cum fidelibus defunctis omnibus in vitam caelestem resurgamus, per Jesum Christum Dominum nostrum.

Deus pro infinita sua clementia Ecclesiae suae concordiam et unitatem concedat, Reginam nostram conservet, pacem regno universo populoque Christiano largiatur, per Jesum Christum Dominum nostrum.

MAGDALENE
CAMBRIDGE (1542)

Ante cibum

Benedic, Domine, nobis et donis tuis, quae de tua largitate sumus sumpturi; et concede ut illis salubriter nutriti tibi debitum obsequium praestare valeamus, per Jesum Christum Dominum et Servatorem nostrum.

Post cibum

VERSICLE   Laus Deo.
RESPONSE   Deo gratias.

The eyes of all wait upon thee, O Lord,
  and thou givest them meat in due season.
Thou openest thine hand
  and fillest every living thing with blessing.

Bless, O Lord, us and thy gifts, which through thy goodness
we are about to receive; and grant that being by them healthfully
nourished, we may be enabled to show our bounden duty toward
thee, through Christ our Lord.

O blessed Trinity, to thee be praise and glory and thanksgiving
  forever.
Let us bless the Father and the Son with the Holy Spirit.
Let us praise and exalt him forever.
Blessed art thou, Lord, in the firmament of heaven,
worthy to be praised, full of glory and exalted evermore.
Magnify the Lord with me
and let us exalt his name together.
Lord, hear my prayer,
and let my cry come unto thee.

Pour, we beseech thee, Lord God, thy grace into our hearts that
we may rightly use to thy glory these gifts of Henry the Eighth
our Founder, Queen Mary, Edward the Third and Hervey de
Stanton, and our other benefactors; and that we may rise again to
heavenly life with those who have departed in the faith of Christ,
through Christ our Lord.

May God through his infinite mercy grant concord and unity
to his Church, and preserve our most serene Queen Elizabeth,
Philip Duke of Edinburgh, the Duke and Duchess of Cornwall,
and all the royal family, and bring peace to the whole realm
and all Christian people.

TRINITY
CAMBRIDGE (1546)

Ante cibum

Oculi omnium in te sperant, Domine,
 Et tu das escam illis in tempore.
Aperis tu manum tuam
 Et imples omne animal benedictione.

Benedic, Domine, nos et dona tua, quae de largitate tua sumus
sumpturi; et concede ut illis salubriter nutriti tibi debitum
obsequium praestare valeamus, per Christum Dominum
nostrum.

Post cibum

Tibi laus, tibi gloria, tibi gratiarum actio in sempiterna saecula,
 O beata Trinitas.
Benedicamus Patrem et Filium cum Spiritu Sancto.
Laudemus et superexaltemus eum in saecula.
Benedictus es, Domine, in firmamento caeli,
Laudabilis et gloriosus et superexaltatus in saecula.
Magnificate Dominum mecum,
Et exaltemus nomen eius in idipsum.
Domine, exaudi orationem meam,
Et clamor meus ad te veniat.

Infunde, quaesumus, Domine Deus, gratiam tuam in mentes
nostras, ut his donis datis ab Henrico Octavo Fundatore nostro,
Regina Maria, Edwardo Tertio et Hervico de Stanton, aliisque
benefactoribus nostris, recte ad tuam gloriam utentes, una cum
illis qui in fide Christi decesserunt ad caelestem vitam resurgamus,
per Christum Dominum nostrum.

 Deus pro sua infinita clementia Ecclesiae suae concordiam et
unitatem concedat, serenissimam Reginam nostram Elizabetham,
Philippum Ducem Edinburgi, Ducem et Ducissem Cornubiae,
totamque regiam familiam conservet, ac pacem regno universo
et omnibus Christianis largiatur.

49

We unhappy and unworthy men do give thee most reverent thanks, almighty God, our heavenly Father, for the victuals which thou hast bestowed on us for the sustenance of the body, at the same time beseeching thee that we may use them soberly, modestly and gratefully. And above all we beseech thee to impart to us the food of angels, the true bread of heaven, the eternal word of God, Jesus Christ our Lord, so that the mind of each of us may feed on him and that through his flesh and blood we may be sustained, nourished and strengthened.

Let all thy works acknowledge thee, O Lord, and let all thy saints bless thee.

Almighty and eternal God, we give thanks to thee for thy favours to all men, for the lord King our first noble Founder, and for the other benefactors of this House; and we beseech thee that, using these gifts aright, we with them may rise again to life in heaven, through Jesus Christ our Lord.

CHRIST CHURCH
OXFORD (1546)

Ante cibum

Nos miseri homines et egeni, pro cibis quos nobis ad corporis
subsidium benigne es largitus, tibi Deus omnipotens, Pater
caelestis, gratias reverenter agimus; simul obsecrantes, ut iis
sobrie, modeste atque grate utamur. Insuper petimus, ut cibum
angelorum, verum panem caelestem, verbum Dei aeternum,
Dominum nostrum Jesum Christum, nobis impertiaris; utque
illo mens nostra pascatur, et per carnem et sanguinem ejus
foveamur, alamur, et corroboremur.

Post cibum (*festal*)

Confiteantur tibi, Domine, omnia opera tua et sancti tui
benedicant tibi.

Omnipotens et aeterne Deus, agimus tibi gratias pro universis
tuis beneficiis, pro domino Fundatore nostro primario,
ceterisque hujus Aedis benefactoribus; et quaesumus ut nos,
his donis recte utentes, una cum illis ad coelestem vitam
resurgamus, per Jesum Christum Dominum nostrum.

Almighty and merciful God, who hast met our needs with thy gifts, make us, following all thy commands in ready and faithful service, carefully to see to whatsoever thou wouldest have done or left undone by us, through Jesus Christ our Lord.

> O Lord, save the Queen,
> and hear us when we call upon thee.

God, in whose hand are the hearts of rulers, who art the comforter of the poor, the strength of the faithful, the protector of all who put their trust in thee, grant to our Queen Elizabeth and to Christian people that they may always acknowledge and worship thee, King of Kings and Lord of Lords, and that after this life they may share in thy eternal Kingdom, through Jesus Christ our Lord.

God, from whom cometh all bounty and goodness, we give thee due thanks that thou shouldest have inspired King Henry the Eighth of that name of blessed memory, to found this Cathedral; and we beseech thee of thy holy mercy that, when through the help of such great benefaction, we have advanced in the praise of thy name, together with all those who are already resting in the Lord, we may obtain blessed resurrection and the rewards of eternal felicity, through Jesus Christ our Lord.

CHRIST CHURCH
OXFORD

Post cibum

Omnipotens et misericors Deus, qui donis tuis nos exsatiasti, effice ut quicquid per nos fieri aut praetermitti velis, diligenter observemus, mandata tua universa prompto atque fideli obsequio obeuntes, per Jesum Christum Dominum nostrum.

ANTIPHON   Domine, salvam fac Reginam.
RESPONSE   Et exaudi nos, quando invocamus te.

Deus, in cujus manu sunt corda regum, qui es humilium consolator, fidelium fortitudo, protector omnium in te sperantium, da Reginae nostrae Elizabethae populoque Christiano ut te Regem regum, et dominantium Dominum, agnoscant semper et venerentur, et post hanc vitam regni tui aeterni fiant participes, per Jesum Christum Dominum nostrum.

Deus, a quo derivatur omnis munificentia et bonitas, debitas tibi gratias agimus, quod felicis memoriae Regem Henricum ejus nominis octavum, ad Ecclesiam hanc fundandam animaveris; et rogamus pro sancta tua misericordia, ut cum nos hoc tanto beneficio adjuti, ad laudem tui nominis profecerimus, una cum omnibus qui jam in Domino dormierunt, beatam resurrectionem, et aeternae felicitatis praemia consequamur, per Jesum Christum Dominum nostrum.

Have mercy upon us, we beseech thee O Lord, and bless thy gifts, of which we are about to partake from thy goodness, through Jesus Christ our Lord.

May the Lord be blessed in his gifts,
    for he is holy in all his works.
Our help is in the name of the Lord,
    who hath made heaven and earth.
May the name of the Lord be blessed,
    as now is and evermore shall be.   Let us pray.

O Lord, preserve Elizabeth our Queen,
    and hear us when we call upon thee.

O Lord God, the resurrection and the life of those who believe, who art always to be praised both by the living and the dead, we give thee thanks for Thomas Pope, Knight, our Founder, and for Elizabeth his wife, both deceased, and for all our benefactors, through whose benevolence we are here maintained in godliness and learning, beseeching thee that, using these thy gifts to thy praise, we may with them proceed to the immortal glory of resurrection, through Jesus Christ our Lord.

TRINITY
OXFORD (1554)

Ante cibum (ferial)

Miserere nostri, te quaesumus Domine, tuisque donis, quae de
tua benignitate percepturi sumus, benedicito, per Jesum
Christum Dominum nostrum.

Ante cibum (festal)[30]

Benedictus sit Deus in donis suis:
    Qui sanctus est in omnibus operibus suis.
Adjutorium nostrum est in nomine Domini:
    Qui fecit caelum et terram.
Sit nomen Domini benedictum:
    Ut nunc est, sic in secula seculorum.   Oremus.

Domine salvam fac Elizabetham Reginam nostram:
    Et exaudi nos, cum invocamus te.

Domine Deus, resurrectio et vita credentium, qui semper es
laudandus cum in viventibus tum etiam in defunctis, agimus tibi
gratias pro Thoma Pope, Milite, Fundatore nostro, et
Elizabetha, consorte ejus, defunctis, ceterisque benefactoribus
nostris, quorum beneficiis hic ad pietatem et ad studia literarum
alimur, rogantes ut nos, his donis ad tuam gloriam recte utentes,
una cum illis ad resurrectionis gloriam immortalem
perducamur, per Jesum Christum Dominum nostrum.

Bless, O Lord, us and these thy gifts, which of thy goodness we are about to receive, through Jesus Christ our Lord.

Our Father, which art in heaven, hallowed be thy name; thy kingdom come; thy will be done, on earth as it is in heaven. Give us this day our daily bread, and forgive us our trespasses as we forgive those who trespass against us. And lead us not into temptation, but deliver us from evil, for thine is the kingdom, the power and the glory, for ever and ever.

May God be blessed in his gifts,
    and holy in all his works.
Our help is in the name of the Lord,
    who hath made heaven and earth.
May the name of the Lord be blessed,
    now and for all ages.

We give thee thanks, almighty and eternal God, for these and all thy benefits; Lord, vouchsafe to have mercy upon us and abide always with us that with the help of the Holy Spirit we may carefully obey thy commandments, through Jesus Christ our Lord.

We give thanks to thee, almighty and eternal God, for Thomas White, Knight, our Founder, deceased, and for Avicia and Joan, his wives, by whose benefits we are here strengthened in godliness and learning, asking that we, using these gifts rightly to thy glory, may with them be led to the immortal glory of resurrection, through Jesus Christ our Lord.

O Lord, preserve the Queen, give peace in our days, and hear us whensoever we call upon thee.

ST JOHN'S
OXFORD (1555)

Ante cibum

Benedic, Domine, nos et haec tua dona quae de tua bonitate
sumus sumpturi: per Jesum Christum Dominum nostrum.

Pater noster, qui es in caelis, sanctificetur nomen tuum; adveniat
regnum tuum; fiat voluntas tua sicut in caelo, sic etiam in terra.
Panem nostrum quotidianum da nobis hodie. Et remitte nobis
debita nostra, sicut nos remittimus debitoribus nostris. Et ne nos
inducas in tentationem, sed libera nos a malo, quia tuum est
regnum, potentia et gloria in saecula saeculorum.

Post cibum

Benedictus sit Deus in donis suis:
  Et sanctus in omnibus operibus suis.
Adjutorium nostrum est in nomine Domini:
  Qui fecit caelum et terram.
Sit nomen Domini benedictum:
  Ex hoc nunc usque in saecula saeculorum.

Agimus tibi gratias, omnipotens et sempiterne Deus, pro his et
universis beneficiis; dignare, Domine, misereri nostrum, et
manere semper nobiscum, ut auxilio Spiritus Sancti mandatis tuis
sedulo obsequamur, per Jesum Christum Dominum nostrum.

or[31]

Agimus tibi gratias, omnipotens et sempiterne Deus, pro Thoma
White, Milite, et Fundatore nostro defuncto, ac Avicia et Joanna
uxoribus ejus, quorum beneficiis hic ad pietatem et ad studia
literarum alimur, rogantes, ut nos, his donis ad tuam gloriam
recte utentes, una cum illis ad resurrectionis gloriam immortalem
perducamur, per Jesum Christum Dominum nostrum.

Response

Serva Reginam, Domine, da pacem in diebus nostris, et exaudi
nos in die quocumque invocamus te.

We wretched and needy men
reverently give thee thanks,
almighty God, heavenly Father,
for the food which thou hast sanctified and bestowed
for the sustenance of the body,
so that we may use it thankfully;
at the same time we beseech thee
that thou wouldst impart to us the food of angels,
the true bread of heaven, the eternal word of God,
Jesus Christ our Lord,
so that our mind may feed on him
and that through his flesh and blood
we may be nourished, sustained and strengthened.

Since, O Lord, almighty and most merciful God,
thou hast satisfied us with thy gifts,
ensure from henceforth that we may diligently regard
what thou wishest to be done or left undone by us
and cause this to be effected with sincere heart,
through Jesus Christ our Lord.

O Lord, keep the Queen safe.
And hear us in the day in which we call on thee.

God, in whose hand are the hearts of Kings,
who art the consoler of the humble
and the courage of the faithful
and protector of all who hope in thee,
grant to our Queen Elizabeth
and to the Christian people
to celebrate wisely the triumph of thy goodness
so that they may be always renewed to glory through thee,
through Jesus Christ our Lord.

JESUS
OXFORD (1571)[32]

Ante cibum

Nos miseri et egentes homines
pro cibo
quem ad alimoniam corporis sanctificatum
nobis es largitus,
ut eo utamur grati
tibi, Deus omnipotens, Pater caelestis,
gratias reverenter agimus;
simul obsecrantes ut cibum angelorum,
verum panem caelestem, verbum Dei aeternum,
Dominum nostrum Jesum Christum
nobis impertiaris,
ut illo mens nostra pascatur
et per carnem et sanguinem ejus
foveamur, alamur et corroboremur.

Post cibum

Quandoquidem nos, Domine, donis tuis,
Omnipotens et misericors Deus, exsatiasti,
effice ut posthac quid per nos fieri aut secus velis
diligenter observemus,
atque illud animo sincero effectum praestemus,
per Jesum Christum Dominum nostrum.

VERSICLE   Domine, salvam fac Reginam.
RESPONSE   Et exaudi nos in die qua invocaverimus te.

Deus, in cuius manu sunt corda regum,
qui es humilium consolator
et fidelium fortitudo
et protector omnium in te sperantium,
da Reginae nostrae Elizabethae
populoque Christiano
triumphum virtutis tuae scienter excolere,
ut per te semper reparentur ad gloriam,
per Christum Dominum nostrum.

The eyes of all wait upon thee, O Lord, and
thou givest them their meat in due season.
Thou openest thine hand
and fillest every living thing with blessing.

Bless, O Lord, us and thy gifts, which of thy bounty we are
about to receive, through Jesus Christ our Lord.

Sanctify us and what is ours, and bless these gifts which of thy
bounty we are about to receive, through Jesus Christ our Lord.

Let all thy works give thanks to thee, O Lord, and let thy saints
bless thee. We give thanks to thee, almighty God, for all thy
goodness, who livest and reignest, God for ever and ever.

To thee be praise and honour and glory for ever and ever,
O blessed and everlasting God.
    We praise thee, most merciful Father, for our most honoured
Founder and for our benefactors, by whose munificence we are
here nurtured to pursue religion and learning, beseeching thee
that, rightly using these gifts to thy glory in this present age, we
may in that which is to come possess with thee that kingdom
which thou hast promised and prepared for them that truly love
thee, through Christ our Lord.
    May God in his infinite mercy grant unity to his Church,
may he preserve our most noble Queen Elizabeth, and bestow
peace upon this realm and upon all Christians.

EMMANUEL
CAMBRIDGE (1584)

Ante cibum

Oculi omnium in te sperant, Domine, et
tu das escam illorum in tempore opportuno.
Aperis tu manum tuam,
et imples omne animal benedictione.

ferial

Benedic, Domine, nos et dona tua, quae de tua largitate sumus
sumpturi, per Jesum Christum Dominum nostrum.

festal

Sanctifica nos et nostra, istisque donis, quae de tua bonitate
sumus sumpturi, benedicito, per Jesum Christum
Dominum nostrum.

Post cibum (*ferial*)

Confiteantur tibi, Domine, omnia opera tua, et sancti tui
benedicant te. Agimus tibi gratias, omnipotens Deus, pro
universis beneficiis tuis, qui vivis et regnas Deus per omnia
saecula saeculorum.

Post cibum (*festal*)

Tibi laus, tibi honor, tibi gloria in omnia saecula, O beate et
sempiterne Deus.

Laudamus te, benignissime Pater, pro honoratissimo
Fundatore nostro et benefactoribus nostris, quorum beneficiis
hic ad pietatem et studia litterarum alimur; orantes te, ut hisce
donis recte ad tuam gloriam utentes in hoc saeculo, tecum in
futuro illud regnum possideamus quod promisisti et praeparasti
vere diligentibus te, per Christum Dominum nostrum.

Deus pro infinita sua clementia Ecclesiae suae unitatem
concedat, augustissimam Reginam nostram Elizabetham
conservet, et pacem universo regno et omnibus Christianis
largiatur.

The eyes of all look toward thee, O Lord; thou givest them their meat in due season. Thou openest thine hand and fillest every living thing with thy blessing.

Sanctify us, we beseech thee, through word and prayer; and give thy blessing to these thy gifts, which of thy bounty we are about to receive, through Jesus Christ our Lord.

We thank thee, omnipotent and eternal God, because, just as by thy ineffable power thou didst create everything, and by thy inscrutable wisdom governest the universe and by thy inexhaustible goodness nourishest all things, so thou dost vouchsafe kindly and generously to give us refreshment at this time. Grant, we beseech thee, Lord, that we thy sons may, in due time, attain with thee that heavenly kingdom which thou hast promised and prepared for those who truly love thee, through Jesus Christ our Lord.

We praise thee, most gracious Father, for our most noble Foundress, the Lady Frances Sidney, Countess of Sussex, and for our supplementary Founders and benefactors, by whose benefactions we are here maintained, to be educated in godliness and learning: beseeching thee that, using these thy gifts rightly and to thy glory in this age, we may, together with thee and the faithful, enjoy life happily in the world to come, through Jesus Christ our Lord.

SIDNEY SUSSEX
CAMBRIDGE (1596)

Ante cibum

Oculi omnium ad te spectant, Domine; tu das eis escam eorum
in tempore opportuno. Aperis tu manum tuam, et imples omne
animal benedictione tua.

Sanctifica nos, quaesumus, per verbum et orationem; istisque
tuis donis, quae de tua bonitate sumus percepturi, benedicito,
per Jesum Christum Dominum nostrum.

Post cibum

Agimus tibi gratias, omnipotens et aeterne Deus, quia, ut tua
ineffabili potentia condidisti omnia, tua inscrutabili sapientia
gubernas universa, et inexhausta bonitate cuncta pascis, sic nos
hoc tempore benigne et liberaliter reficere dignatus es. Largire
nobis, quaesumus, Domine, filiis tuis, ut tecum aliquando
coeleste illud regnum possideamus, quod promisisti et
praeparasti vere diligentibus te, per Jesum Christum Dominum
nostrum.

Laudamus te, benignissime Pater, pro nobilissima Fundatrice
nostra Domina Francisca Sidney, Sussexiae Comitissa, pro
Fundatoribus accessoriis et benefactoribus nostris, quorum
beneficiis hic ad pietatem et studia literarum alimur: orantes te,
ut his tuis donis recte ad tuam gloriam utentes in hoc saeculo,
te una cum fidelibus in futuro feliciter perfruamur, per Jesum
Christum Dominum nostrum.

Blessed be God for his gifts,
who is holy in all his works.

Our help is in the name of the Lord,
who made heaven and earth.

Blessed be the name of the Lord
from henceforth and for evermore.

O Lord, save Queen Elizabeth
and hear us when we call upon thee.

O Lord God, the life and resurrection of believers,
who art always to be praised both by the living
and by the dead, we give thee thanks for Nicholas
Wadham Esquire, and his wife Dorothy, our
departed Founders, and for our other benefactors,
by whose gifts we are here nurtured to godliness
and learning, and we pray that, making the right
use of these thy gifts, we may be brought together
with them to the resurrection of glory, through
Jesus Christ our Lord.

WADHAM

OXFORD (1610)

Ante cibum

SCHOLAR Benedictus sit Deus in donis suis.
WARDEN Sanctus in omnibus operibus suis.

SCHOLAR Adjutorium nostrum in nomine Domini.
WARDEN Qui fecit coelum et terras.

SCHOLAR Sit nomen Dei benedictum.
WARDEN Ex hoc usque in saecula saeculorum.

SCHOLAR Domine salvam fac Elizabetham Reginam.
WARDEN Et exaudi nos cum invocamus te.

SCHOLAR Domine Deus, vita et resurrectio credentium,
qui semper es laudandus, tum in viventibus, tum
in defunctis, agimus tibi gratias pro Nicolao
Wadhamo Armigero, et Dorothea uxore ejus,
Fundatoribus nostris defunctis, aliisque
benefactoribus nostris, quorum beneficiis hic ad
pietatem et ad studium litterarum alimur, rogantes
ut nos, his tuis donis recte utentes, una cum illis
ad resurrectionem gloriam[33] perducamur, per
Jesum Christum Dominum nostrum.

For this food, which thou hast sanctified and granted to us for the nourishment of our body, we reverently give thee thanks, almighty Father, at the same time beseeching thee to impart to us the food of angels, the true heavenly bread, the eternal word of God, Jesus Christ our Lord, so that the mind of each of us may feed on him and that by his body and blood we may be nourished, supported and strengthened.

We give thee thanks, merciful God, for the nurture we have received by thy goodness; earnestly beseeching thee that thou will keep safe our most serene Queen, all the royal family and thy whole people and ever guard them in the safety of peace.

PEMBROKE
OXFORD (1624)

Ante cibum

Pro hoc cibo, quem ad alimonium corporis nostri sanctificatum
es largitus, nos tibi, Pater omnipotens, reverenter gratias agimus,
simul obsecrantes ut cibum angelorum, panem verum coelestem,
Dei verbum aeternum, Jesum Christum Dominum nostrum
nobis impertiare, ut eo mens nostra pascatur, et per carnem et
sanguinem ejus alamur, foveamur, corroboremur.

Post cibum[34]

Gratias tibi agimus, Deus misericors, pro acceptis a tua bonitate
alimentis; enixe comprecantes ut serenissimam nostram
Reginam Elizabetham, totam regiam familiam, populumque
tuum universum, tuta in pace semper custodias.

We unhappy and unworthy men do give thee most reverent thanks, almighty God, our heavenly Father, for the victuals which thou hast bestowed on us for the sustenance of the body, at the same time beseeching thee that we may use them soberly, modestly and gratefully. And above all we beseech thee to impart to us the food of angels, the true bread of heaven, the eternal word of God, Jesus Christ our Lord, so that the mind of each of us may feed on him and that through his flesh and blood we may be sustained, nourished and strengthened.

Almighty and merciful God, who hast met our needs with thy gifts, make us, following all thy commands in ready and faithful service, carefully to see to whatsoever thou wouldest have done or left undone by us, through Jesus Christ our Lord.

> O Lord, save the Queen
> and hear us when we call upon thee.

We give thee thanks, almighty and everlasting God, for Sir Thomas Cookes, Baronet, our Founder, by whose benefits we are here nourished in godliness and learning. At the same time we ask that, using these gifts aright to thy glory, we may together with him be led to the immortal glory of resurrection, through Jesus Christ our Lord.

WORCESTER
OXFORD (1714)

Ante cibum

Nos miseri homines et egeni, pro cibis quos nobis ad corporis
subsidium benigne es largitus, tibi Deus omnipotens, Pater
caelestis, gratias reverenter agimus; simul obsecrantes, ut iis
sobrie, modeste atque grate utamur. Insuper petimus, ut cibum
angelorum, verum panem caelestem, verbum Dei aeternum,
Dominum nostrum Jesum Christum, nobis impertiaris: utque
illo mens nostra pascatur, et per carnem et sanguinem ejus
foveamur, alamur, et corroboremur.

Post cibum

Omnipotens et misericors Deus, qui donis tuis nos exsatiasti,
effice ut quicquid per nos fieri aut praetermitti velis, diligenter
observemus, mandata tua universa prompto atque fideli obsequio
obeuntes, per Jesum Christum Dominum nostrum.

ANTIPHON   Domine, salvam fac Reginam.
RESPONSE   Et exaudi nos quando invocamus te.

Agimus tibi gratias, omnipotens et sempiterne Deus, pro Thoma
Cookesio, Baronetto, Fundatore nostro, cujus beneficio hic ad
pietatem, studiumque literarum alimur: simul rogantes ut, his
donis ad tuam gloriam recte utentes, una cum eo ad
resurrectionis gloriam immortalem perducamur, per Jesum
Christum Dominum nostrum.

Bless, O Lord, us and thy gifts,
which from thy bounty we are about to receive,
and grant that being by them healthfully nourished
we may be enabled to show our bounden duty toward thee.

Praise be to God.
Thanks be to God.

Bless us, O Lord, and all members of this college, and also thy
gifts, which of thy bounty we are about to receive; and having
been wholesomely nourished by the same let us dutifully render
to thee the thanks that are owed. Protect, we beseech thee, O
Lord, thy sons and daughters and provide for the needs both of
our souls and bodies, at this present time and for evermore.

The eyes of all wait upon thee, O Lord, and thou providest their
meat in due season. Thou openest thine hand, and fillest every
living thing with blessing.

Have mercy upon us, we beseech thee, O Lord, and bless thy
gifts, which from thy kindness we are about to receive, through
Jesus Christ our Lord.

DOWNING
CAMBRIDGE (1800)

Ante cibum

Benedic, Domine, nos et dona tua,
quae de tua largitate sumus sumpturi,
et concede ut illis salubriter nutriti
tibi debitum obsequium praestare valeamus.

Post cibum

ANTIPHON Laus Deo.
RESPONSE Deo gratias.

GIRTON
CAMBRIDGE (1869)

Ante cibum

Benedic, Domine, nobis et omnibus hujus collegii alumnis,
donisque tuis quae de munificentia tua sumus jam sumpturi; et
illis salubriter nutriti debitas tibi gratias pie reddamus. Custodi,
quaesumus, Domine, filios et filias et consule necessitatibus
animarum et corporum, hoc ipso momento et in aeternum.[35]

KEBLE
OXFORD (1870)

Ante cibum

Oculi omnium in te sperant, Domine, et tu das escam illorum
in tempore opportuno. Aperis tu manum tuam, et imples omne
animal benedictione tua.

Miserere nostri, te quaesumus, Domine. Tuisque donis quae
de tua benignitate sumus percepturi benedicito, per Jesum
Christum Dominum nostrum.

Bless us, Lord God, and these gifts, which of thy bounty
we are about to receive, through Jesus Christ our Lord.

We give thee thanks, almighty God, for these thy gifts to us all,
which we receive from thy bounty, who livest and reignest and
art our God for ever.

Bless, O Lord, us and thy gifts, which through thy bounty
we are about to receive; and grant that we may use these thy
favours to thy praise, and enjoy them with grateful hearts,
through Jesus Christ our Lord.

Blessed art thou O Lord God, king and creator of the world,
who brought forth bread and green herbs from the earth
for our use, and who hast preserved us to this present hour.
Thou fillest all living things with thy blessing.

We give thanks to thee, O God, ruler and maker of the universe,
for that thou hast from thy great goodness fed us when we were
hungry; and grant that we, strengthened by these thy gifts, may
have power to do all things that are good, to thy glory.

NEWNHAM
CAMBRIDGE (1871)

Ante cibum

Benedic nobis, Domine Deus, et his donis, quae ex liberalitate
tua sumpturae[36] sumus,per Jesum Christum Dominum nostrum.

Post cibum

Gratias tibi agimus, omnipotens Deus, pro his et universis donis
tuis, quae de tua largitate accepimus, qui vivis et regnas et es
Deus, in saecula saeculorum.

SELWYN
CAMBRIDGE (1882)

Ante cibum

Benedic, Domine, nobis et donis tuis, quae de tua largitate
sumus sumpturi; et concede ut iis muneribus tuis ad laudem
tuam utamur, gratisque animis fruamur, per Jesum Christum
Dominum nostrum.

HUGHES HALL
CAMBRIDGE (1885)

Ante prandiam

Benedictus es, Domine Deus, Rex et Artifex mundi,
qui cibum e terra herbamque viridem hominum in usum eduxisti,
quique usque in horam hanc novissimam nos servasti.
Omne animal imples benedictione.

Post prandiam

Gratias tibi agimus, Domine Deus, Rex et Artifex mundi,
quoniam ex tua largitate esurientes nos implevisti,
et concede ut his tuis donis salubriter nutriti,
omnia bona ad gloriam tuam facere valeamus.

Bless us, Lord God, and these gifts, which of thy bounty
we are about to receive, through Jesus Christ our Lord.

Bless, O Lord, us and these thy gifts, which of thy goodness
we are about to receive, through Jesus Christ our Lord.

We give thee thanks, O almighty God, for all thy benefits,
who livest and reignest for ever and ever.

Almighty and everlasting God, who through thy only-begotten
Son, after his glorious resurrection, didst refresh with food the
blessed Apostle Peter, and didst earnestly command him to feed
thy flock; may these thy gifts, we beseech thee, serve for our
refreshment, and may thy grace feed us for our sanctification,
through the same Christ our Lord.

ST HUGH'S
OXFORD (1886)

Ante cibum

Benedic nobis, Domine Deus, et his donis, quae ex liberalitate tua sumpturi sumus, per Jesum Christum Dominum nostrum.

ST BENET'S HALL
OXFORD (1897)

Ante cibum

Benedic, Domine, nos et haec tua dona, quae de tua largitate sumus sumpturi, per Jesum Christum Dominum nostrum.

Post cibum

Agimus tibi gratias, omnipotens Deus, pro universis beneficiis tuis, qui vivis et regnas in saecula saeculorum.

ST PETER'S
OXFORD (1929)

Ante cibum

Omnipotens sempiterne Deus, qui per unigenitum Filium tuum post gloriosam ejus resurrectionem beatum Petrum apostolum prandio refecisti et gregem tuum pascere instantius praecepisti; proficiant nobis, quaesumus, haec tua dona ad refectionem, et pascat nos gratia tua ad sanctificationem, per eundem Christum Dominum nostrum.

Let us render proper thanks to God.

Bless, O Lord, us and thy gifts, which from thy bounty
we are about to receive, and grant that being by them
healthfully nourished we may be enabled to show
our bounden duty, through Christ our Lord.

Be present with us, O Lord our God: and grant that those of the
Holy Cross whom thou makest to rejoice thou mayest also
nourish by wholesome gifts, through our Lord Jesus Christ.

We give thanks to thee, O Lord, for all thy favours
through our Lord Jesus Christ.

ST ANNE'S
OXFORD (1952)

Ante cibum

Quas decet Deo gratias agamus.

CHURCHILL
CAMBRIDGE (1960)

Ante cibum

Benedic, Domine, nos et dona tua, quae de largitate tua
sumus sumpturi, et concede ut illis salubriter nutriti
tibi debitum obsequium praestare valeamus,
per Jesum Dominum nostrum.

ST CROSS
OXFORD (1965)

Ante cibum

Adesto nobis, Domine Deus noster: et concede ut quos Sanctae
Crucis laetari facis honore, ejus donis quoque salutaribus nutrias,
per Dominum nostrum Jesum Christum.

Post cibum

Gratias agimus tibi, Domine, pro omnibus beneficiis tuis
per Dominum nostrum Jesum Christum.

Bless, O Lord
Us and your gifts
Which from thy bounty we are about to receive,
And grant that being by them healthfully nourished
We may be enabled to show our bounden duty toward thee.
Through Christ our Lord.

The eyes of all wait upon thee, O Lord, and thou givest them meat in due season. Thou openest thine hand and fillest every living thing with blessing. Bless, O Lord, us and thy gifts, which through thy goodness we are about to receive.

Praise be to God.
Thanks be to God.

Bless, O Lord, us and your gifts,
through Jesus Christ our Lord.

WOLFSON
CAMBRIDGE (1965)

Ante cibum (festal)

Benedic, Domine
Nos et dona tua
Quae de largitate tua sumus sumpturi
Et concede ut illis salubriter nutriti
Tibi debitum obsequium praestare valeamus
Per Christum Dominum nostrum.

FITZWILLIAM
CAMBRIDGE (1966)

Ante cibum

Oculi omnium in te sperant, Domine, et tu das escam illorum
in tempore opportuno. Aperis tu manum tuam et imples omne
animal benedictione. Benedic Domine nos et dona tua quae de
tua largitate suus sumpturi.

Post cibum

Laus Deo.
Deo gratias.

ROBINSON
CAMBRIDGE (1977)

Ante cibum

Benedic Domine nobis et donis tuis,
per Jesum Christum Dominum nostrum.

Eternal God, as we meet together in the fellowship of this meal, we remember the gifts and blessing we have received, and are thankful for them. May we learn to use them to their fullest measure, for the good of the whole world.

No good thing is worth having unless you have someone to share it with.

For this food and for the fellowship of this college, we praise thee, O God.

For all your gifts we give thanks.

HARRIS MANCHESTER
OXFORD (1990)[37]

Ante cibum

Domine aeterne, dum convenimus huius convivii societate
coniuncti, eorum munerum et beneficiorum memores quae abs
te accepimus, gratias tibi agimus. Da nobis ut his donis quam
saluberrime utamur, ita ut haec omni terrarum orbi conducant.

MANSFIELD
OXFORD (1995)

Ante cibum

Nullius boni possessio est iucunda sine socio.

GREEN TEMPLETON
OXFORD (2008)

Ante cibum

Pro hoc cibo et sodalitate hujus collegii te Deum laudamus.

Post cibum

Pro omnibus donis gratias agimus.

THE TWO-WORD GRACE

Ante cibum

Benedictus benedicat.

May the Blessed One give a blessing.

This is the standard grace, *ferial* or *festal*, used at the following colleges:

OXFORD

Hertford (1874)	Nuffield (1937)
Lady Margaret Hall (1878)	St Antony's (1950)
Somerville (1879)	Linacre (1962)
St Hilda's (1893)	Wolfson (1966)
St Catherine's (1962)	

It is also used at Balliol, Exeter, New College, Magdalen, Mansfield and St Edmund Hall, and occasionally elsewhere.

CAMBRIDGE

Homerton (1824)	Lucy Cavendish (1965)
Murray Edwards (1954)	Darwin (1964)
Wolfson (1965)	

It is an alternative grace at Pembroke.

Post cibum

Benedicto benedicatur.

either　Let praise be given to the Blessed One.
or　Let a blessing be given by the Blessed One.

These alternatives are discussed on page xvi.

In use *passim* in both universities.

ASSOCIATED CUSTOMS
AT DINNER

Seating

S TATUS and seniority of membership used to be reflected in an
order of precedence at dinner. Not so long ago scholars sat at
separate tables from commoners, and in the days of *superioris ordinis
commensales* (gentlemen or fellow commoners old style) a special
table was provided for them. There is generally now no special
seating other than at High Table.

Access to this is often possible through a convenient adjacent
door, but the procession of dons and their guests sometimes
enters the hall through the screens at the other end. Their seating,
such as still obtains in many halls below the dais, was probably
originally on benches, though a special chair would have been
placed for the head of the house at the end of the table beneath
an oriel window. In some colleges this has remained the seat of
honour, which elsewhere is in the centre of the table facing the
body of the hall.

Readings from the scriptures

While statutes in many colleges make no reference to grace,
several are explicit on the subject of a reading during the meal
in Latin of a chapter or 'convenient portion of Holy Scripture', a
practice from which the title Bible Clerk is derived. During this
'all are to sit, modestly, becomingly, with their caps on their heads,
according to their condition reverently and silently'. *Lectiones* are
now to be heard only in the refectories of a few religious houses,
where the readings are not nowadays in Latin and are not always
from the Bible.

Toasting

Two hundred years ago Parson Woodforde in his progress from scholar to sub-warden at New College describes the fare and the formalities of dining.[38] Some of these remain unchanged and dinner jackets are still to be seen on a Sunday at High Table in a few halls because it is the weekly feast-day. The medieval tradition continues of drinking in a 'grace' cup to the health of others – *in memoriam absentium* or *in salutem praesentium*. The *poculum caritatis* (loving cup) circulates on the days of great Church festivals or where there is other cause for celebration, with three people standing at any one time, one of them drinking with companions on either side for protection. At feasts and gaudies the commemoration of founders and benefactors remains of great significance – *in piam memoriam Fundatoris nostri et benefactorum nostrorum*. If they are not remembered in a grace, this omission can be redressed in a toast.

The sconce cup, which was once associated with penalties for such misdemeanours as false quantities in the reading of grace, can also be used for more informal toasting. When P.S. Allen was elected President of Corpus Christi at Oxford in 1924 he returned to his former college: 'I dined in Merton ... by request, the young men sent me up a sconce of beer and gave me a really charming ovation, with smiling applause all over the hall, to which I replied by rising in my place and drinking out of my sconce and bowing to them all. After which I sent them sconces of beer too. Wasn't that a pretty compliment?'[39]

Many colleges possess other valuable pieces of plate and at formal dinners there is circulation of the rose-water dish. A basin and ewer were once practical and hygienic accompaniments at table.

Withdrawal from the hall

College statutes often include a direction that there was to be no lingering in the hall and that those *in statu pupillari* were to return to their rooms for study. The hour of *prandium* gradually advanced but the rule remained. Although the hall was the centre of the community life of the college, the rule applied also in respect of *coena* except for specially arranged meetings or social gatherings. In the eighteenth century these began to take place in combination or common rooms.

Within living memory an undergraduate representative had to ask permission from High Table before those at his table could withdraw. This was automatically extended to the remainder. Now with the departure of the majority, the fellows finish their meal in a quieter hall before withdrawing to the privacy of their chambers after a concluding *Gratiarum Actio*.

NOTES

1. J. Jones, *A History of Balliol College 1263–1939* (Oxford 1988), p. 282.
2. *Statutes of the Colleges of Oxford*, reprinted for the Royal Commission of 1853, Pembroke 11 *De prandio, coena et refectionibus*.
3. I Timothy IV. 4–5. I Corinthians X. 31.
4. The *post prandium* grace shows the original reference in its second petition to King Charles I as the reigning monarch when the broadsheet was printed. The preliminary sentences shown in the picture may have been said antiphonally. If so, the document illustrates old and new forms of grace then in use.
5. F. Madan, *Oxford outside the Guide Books* (Oxford 1923), p. 117.
6. Jones, *A History of Balliol College*, p. 213.
7. James Stuart, *Reminiscences* (London 1911), p. 143.
8. H.A. Wilson, *The Gelasian Sacramentary* (Oxford 1894), pp. 293–4.
9. *Breviarium Romanum* (London 1946) pp. 234–5.
10. H.L. Dixon, *'Saying Grace' Historically Considered* (Oxford 1903) p. 161.
11. W.H. Frere, *The Use of Sarum* (Cambridge 1898) vol. I, pp. 242–7.
12. *Liber Precum Publicarum in usum Ecclesiae Cathedralis Christi Oxoniae*, 1660. The College was constitutionally part of the Cathedral until 1867, the whole as *Aedes* ('the House') *Christi* (see p. 51).
13. *Private Prayers of the reign of Queen Elizabeth 1564*. Parker Society Reprint, vol. 43 (London 1851). *Preces privatae* are part of this volume, pp. 399–402.
14. W.H. Stevenson and H.E. Salter, *The Early History of St John's College Oxford* (Oxford 1939), p. 21, where there is a reference in a footnote to R. Hospinianus, *De origine et progressu monachatus* (Zürich 1587), folio 179v.
15. E. Bradley, *The Adventures of Mr Verdant Green 1853–6* by Cuthbert Bede B.A. (Edinburgh) cap. 6, p. 52, reissued Oxford 1982.
16. Dixon, *'Saying Grace'*, pp. 162–97 contains a record of Oxford graces, which P. Bliss added to *Reliquiae Hearnianae* (London 1857), 2 vols, Appendix V. Note that the collection of graces was made not by Thomas Hearne, but by Philip Bliss.
17. *Benedictus sit Deus in donis suis*. This is the opening line of a series of four couplets used as part of an antiphonal grace. Each line is an extract from a verse in the Psalms. The customary punctuation of the Latin texts has been followed. It became known as the 'Winchester' grace because it was set to music there by John Reading (d. 1692). It is now one of the anthems popular at feasts.
18. *Oculi omnium in te sperant*. These are the opening words of Psalm 145 vv. 14–15. Alternative verbs to *sperant* (used in the Vulgate Ps. 144) are *spectant, aspiciunt, respiciunt*.
19. *Benedic, Domine, dona tua quae de largitate sumus sumpturi*. This is the original text in the *Gelasian Sacramentary*, on which some extended versions of this grace have been based. Variations exist to this text, both grammatical and verbal:
    (i) *Benedic* is followed by the dative in a majority of the graces and is occasionally used in the subjunctive.
    (ii) Five alternatives are found to *largitate* – *benignitate, bonitate, gratia, liberalitate, munificentia*.
    (iii) The preposition preceding these nouns is either *de* or *ex*.
    The second petition about 'our bounden duty' is found only in Cambridge.
20. *Deus est caritas*. I John IV. 16.
21. P. Simpson, *The Oriel Record* (1940), pp. 242–3. This is a translation reputedly by Erasmus in his *Convivium Religiosum* of a grace recorded by St John Chrysostom ('the golden mouthed one') as being widely in use among Greek-speaking Christians. Erasmus (1469 – 1536) visited Oxford in 1499 and Cambridge in 1505. He was in Cambridge again

between 1511 and 1514 as Lady Margaret's Reader in Divinity. Most of his writing was done towards the end of his life.

22. St Edmund Hall, which is the sole survivor of a former group of private halls in Oxford, had a connection with the neighbouring Queen's College for some four hundred years until 1957.

23. Erasmus is also credited with the words *Quicquid appositum est aut apponetur.* S.C. Roberts, *Adventures with Authors* (Cambridge 1966), p. 187 records that the grace was introduced in his Mastership in about 1948. The second half of each petition is a translation into Latin of words of an English eighteenth century grace.

24. *Mensae caelestis nos participes facias, Rex aeternae gloriae.* cf. I Corinthians X 21. This is sometimes used as a prefatory prayer.

25. Magdalen at Oxford has a large collection of festal graces. Its 'Customary', a procedural handbook, contains ceremonial instructions for the President, the Fellows, the Demies and the Choir at the 'Commemoration of Simon Perrot' and the 'Restoration' dinner.

26. *Pater noster, qui es in caelis...* Matthew VI.9–13.

27. S.J. Mitchell, 'Cambridge College Graces' in *Cambridge*, the magazine of the Cambridge Society no. 24 (1989), p. 34. He noted that this was possibly the oldest ferial prayer before dinner. It is traditionally thought to have been written by Bishop Fisher (1469–1535) on the refoundation of Christ's College by Lady Margaret Beaufort.

28. Brasenose has a similar set of four graces. Note the comparison with the *ante coenam* grace at Christ's – 'nothing bears odour' and 'nothing is sweet or pleasant'. This grace is said at BNC on Shrove Tuesday and on 1 June (the anniversary of the laying of the foundation stone).

29. The last couplet in the *ante cibum* grace, generally known as the Lesser Doxology, is most appropriate to this College. The unusual words *in idipsum* at the end of the eighth line of the *post cibum* grace are to be found in the Vulgate Psalm 33 v. 3.

30. The festal grace is said at the season of Trinity, its first part in the form of a duologue between the President and the senior scholar, who makes the responses. The concluding collect is said every Sunday in term time at the end of Evensong in Chapel in an English translation.

31. One of the alternative petitions is made at the 'Richard Rawlinson' dinner, and the other at the 'Sir Thomas White' dinner and at gaudies.

32. These graces are reproduced as set out on a card for use of the scholar on duty, with possible phrasing in mind. The translation was by J.G. Griffith, Fellow of the college and Public Orator from 1973 to 1980.

33. *ad resurrectionis gloriam* – 'to the glory of the resurrection' – would seem to make better sense than *'ad resurrectionem glorias'*, the form recorded by Philip Bliss in 1857. See n16.

34. *T. Hearne, Collections*, ed. C.E. Doble. (Oxford 1888), vol. III, p. 90, 16 December 1710: 'Mr Camden when he was a very young man of Broad Gate Hall now Pembroke College made the Latin grace which they use to this day'. William Camden (1551–1623) studied in Oxford from 1566 to 1571.

Boswell's *Life of Samuel Johnson*, ed. G.B. Hill and L.F. Powell (Oxford 1934–64), vol. V, p. 482. Dr Johnson recited this grace from memory in 1773 at the University of St Andrews, where a grace in Latin was subsequently adopted and continues in use.

35. This was the text of the grace as composed and set to music for two voices about 1950. Now that men have been admitted to the College, the feminine endings of four words have been changed.

36. *sumpturi* if there are men present.

37. J. Woodforde, *The Diary of a Country Parson 1758–1802* (Oxford 1978), 25 December 1773, pp. 85–7.

38. H.M. Allen, *Letters of P.S. Allen* (Oxford 1939), p. 218.

39. Manchester, a Unitarian foundation, became a college of Oxford University in 1996 and devised this grace on achieving that status.

COLLEGES AND HALLS

WHERE A GRACE IS SAID IN LATIN

CAMBRIDGE

Christ's, 39, 41
Churchill, 77
Clare, 11
Corpus Christi, 19
Darwin, 82
Downing, 71
Emmanuel, 61
Fitzwilliam, 79
Girton, 71
Gonville and Caius, 17
Homerton, 82
Hughes Hall, 73
Jesus, 37
King's, 25, 27
Lucy Cavendish, 82

Magdalene, 47
Murray Edwards, 82
Newnham, 73
Pembroke, 15
Peterhouse, 7
Queens', 29
Robinson, 79
St Catharine's, 35
St John's, 45
Selwyn, 73
Sidney Sussex, 63
Trinity, 49
Trinity Hall, 19
Wolfson, 79

OXFORD

All Souls, 25
Balliol, 5
Brasenose, 43
Christ Church, 51, 53
Corpus Christi, 47
Exeter, 9
Green Templeton, 81
Harris Manchester, 81
Hertford, 82
Jesus, 59
Keble, 71
Lady Margaret Hall, 82
Linacre, 82
Lincoln, 23
Magdalen, 31, 33
Mansfield, 81
Merton, 7
New College, 21
Nuffield, 82

Oriel, 9
Pembroke, 67
The Queen's, 13
St Anne's, 77
St Antony's, 82
St Benet's Hall, 75
St Catherine's, 82
St Cross, 77
St Edmund Hall, 15
St Hilda's, 82
St Hugh's, 75
St John's, 57
St Peter's, 75
Somerville, 82
Trinity, 55
University, 3
Wadham, 65
Wolfson, 82
Worcester, 69